OUTBID

OUTBID

David Hume

HEINEMANN: LONDON

William Heinemann Ltd,
10 Upper Grosvenor Street, London W1X 9PA

LONDON MELBOURNE TORONTO
JOHANNESBURG AUCKLAND

SBN 434 35450 3

Photoset by Rowland Phototypesetting Ltd,
Bury St Edmunds, Suffolk
Printed and bound in Great Britain by
Redwood Burn Limited, Trowbridge, Wiltshire

For Lucinda as Doreen

Chapter I

"On the whole we're not very optimistic about British interest rates. Milton Friedman has been a consultant of ours for some years now and everything we hear from him convinces us that the Federal Reserve means business and until rates come down there, ours will have to stay up." As James Murray listened to himself regurgitating Braithwaites' conventional wisdom for that day's clutch of luncheon guests, investment managers from the insurance companies and pension funds, he blessed again the alchemy of an ancient name in the City of London which could change such commonplace thought into wisdom. His guests, who between them were responsible for the investment of billions of pounds, believed themselves to be shrewd and perceptive. In their newspapers and the brokers' circulars brought daily in dozens to their desks they must have read the banal point he had just made countless times, but the fact that it had been said in this dignified, panelled room graced with fine paintings and old silver gave it a significance the printed word could no longer hold for them. Was it the authority of long history? Or might it just be plain snobbishness?

"Yes, but once economic activity begins to slacken there . . ." The man from the Providential infelicitously combined dullness and length in his arguments. James dutifully assumed an expression of interest while he assessed the chances of his wife Clarissa's Pekinese being well enough to allow her to go to the new production of *Rigoletto* that night:

on occasions he wished that one of the ill-tempered creature's periodic maladies would prove fatal. Before he had reached a conclusion on its current survival chances, the sanctity of the lunch room was softly violated by a discreet half-volume ring from the telephone in the corner. Braithwaites held that the social demands of lunch took precedence over the commercial demands of the stock market, except in cases of dire urgency. With a muttered "Do excuse me, please," James took the call. It was the lunchtime duty partner: "James, forgive me interrupting lunch but I thought you ought to know that the market has been hit by an astonishing announcement from Blenders. They say they're probably going to make a loss this year and that they will only pay a token dividend."

"Good Lord. What's the price done?"

"It's been marked down from 230p to 180p. And as Blenders is one of the shares in the *Financial Times* Index, it's off by five points."

"What an extraordinary thing: we'd better find out quickly what's behind it. See if you can discover where Milo is lunching and ask him to get back as soon as is decently possible and contact his Uncle Andrew at the company."

As James returned to the table, the man from the Providential was droning to a lame close. "Forgive me changing the subject, but there has been something of a bombshell from Blenders. They say there will probably be no profit this year and that the dividend is in danger. It has knocked the price by 50p."

The director of the Mogul Pension Fund seized the conversational initiative: "I've often wondered about their management," he said sententiously.

"Blenders is really no more than a loose federation of the big Scottish whisky companies. They still behave like family businesses and from all I hear there's precious little financial control from the centre. If you ask me," (this was his favourite conversational device and carried the unspoken implication that the others had erred in failing to seek his opinion sooner) "it was only a matter of time before one of them came a cropper and got the whole group into trouble. But, James, you're the brokers to Blenders: this can't have come as a total shock to you?"

A little nettled that a gap in Braithwaites fabled intelligence system was apparent, James had to concede that it had. The role of broker to a company is an ambiguous but important strand in the web of financial relationships which bind the City to its clients. The basic function is to advise a company whenever it wants to raise money by issuing shares: out of this has developed a general liaison, which extends to keeping major shareholders in touch with the company's financial health. The prohibitions on share dealing by those in the know, 'insiders' in stock market jargon, make the current state of that health a matter of particular delicacy. Too clear a danger signal could be construed as a breach of ethics. The City, ever adaptable, has evolved its own semaphore code: "Things aren't going too badly" means that the trend of the recent past continues but "I'd wait till we see the profits" is a clear warning that the figures could be nasty.

Braithwaites are brokers not only to Blenders but to most of the major companies in Britain, a position achieved through probity, long history, and an unchallenged place at the heart of the financial Establishment. It is a position maintained by the partners being on first-name terms with the two hundred or so men who run Britain's major companies: to admit ignorance of Blenders' disastrous change in fortune was for James doubly galling. His assistant, Milo Cavendish-Hume, was the nephew of a Blenders' director, Andrew MacLintock, and Milo had given no hint that Blenders faced problems.

"You may be right about their financial controls," said James guardedly, "it certainly sounds to me as though a problem in one subsidiary has caught the Group unawares. We shall do our best to have a word with them this afternoon and we'll be in touch afterwards."

James then skilfully steered the conversation into more general channels by commenting on the poor management record of Scottish companies generally, a hoary (and well-documented) theme but one, given the prevalence of Scots among the fund management fraternity, guaranteed to provoke debate. The tactic succeeded and lunch ended without further discussion of Blenders' woes.

Back at his desk in the partners' room, James promptly sent for Milo. Braithwaites still retained a large, light, panelled room for its five managing partners, hung with portraits of their predecessors. This working arrangement could make concentration difficult on occasions, but it did ensure that all were broadly in touch with the day's business. Although second partner, James was effectively in charge of that business: his senior partner, Giles Barnaby, was in line to become Lord Mayor and had developed a full, if unproductive, life devoted largely to his livery company, the City Corporation, the Council of the Stock Exchange, numerous charities and various bodies devoted, in a generalised way, to improving international relations. His partners liked to say wryly that if an Anglo-Eskimo society were formed, Giles would be an automatic choice for the committee. Still, James did not object to the arrangement: it left him in unchallenged charge and he knew that his relish for quick decisions made him more effective than Giles.

Milo entered the room looking as though he had for once exerted himself. "Sorry I couldn't get back sooner. I was lunching with the Foreign and Commonwealth and their venture capital man is very excited about a high performance motor-scooter which uses hardly any petrol and which he says will outsell the Japanese if . . ."

". . . if the British worker can be persuaded to make it," James finished the sentence for him. "We can talk about that later. Milo, what on earth is going on at Blenders?"

"I saw the announcement on the tape. Bit of a shock I must say."

"It's extremely serious and, with respect, Milo, it shouldn't have caught us completely unawares. Didn't Andrew mention anything to you? After all he is your uncle and we are the company's brokers. I grant you he doesn't do that much for his director's fees but even he should have known that something was amiss."

Milo rearranged his long limbs into a brisker position. He was fond of his uncle and when he had tried to telephone him a fortnight earlier at the end of January, Andrew had been away at his ski resort development in the French Alps. Although Andrew, like Milo himself, was at best moderately conscientious, Milo felt it safe to assume that even his uncle would not go away if anything were seriously amiss, so thought it fair to reply, "I had the impression that everything was in very good order."

"Then it's time, Milo, you got your impression up-to-date." James ran Braithwaites by suggestion rather than command and this came as close to a rebuke as his style allowed. But in its way it was more effective than a tirade from a hectorer.

"Yes. I see. You're quite right. I'll get on with it straight away."

"Blenderrrs," said the voice with a gentle burr. "Misterr MacLintock? He's still in the Board meeting, Mr Cavendish-Hume. I'll get him to call you back."

Blenders' Adam mansion dominates the grey Georgian elegance of Charlotte Square as surely as the company bestrides the whisky trade: inside, its pillared, high-ceilinged hall and knot of messengers at the mahogany reception desk assert the easy self-confidence of an unchallenged commercial ruler. But around the great oval table in the boardroom – once the ballroom where Edinburgh society gathered in the days of David Hume and Adam Smith – that collective self-confidence was cracking. For the Board, which normally met once a quarter at noon to ratify swiftly the policies of the paid executives before turning to more important matters such as the shooting calendar, had been wrangling since ten o'clock.

The Chairman, the Earl of Glencorres, KG, GCMG, GCVO, DSO, Hon DCL, was finding the whole affair grossly distasteful. After a distinguished career in the Army, the Diplomatic Service and at Court, the Blenders job had been arranged to supplement his pension and provide him with a car, chauffeur, London flat and expenses. His role, he had been assured, would be largely representational and at most would involve acting as referee between the rival factions of the Board, who still jealously preserved their autonomy. It also gave him the opportunity, in which he found a good craftsman's satisfaction, of exercising his talent to get through an agenda speedily and tactfully. Today that tact had been fully stretched and the raw emotions around the table provoked in him a nostalgic twinge for the better constructed arguments and more artfully concealed malice he had known in the Foreign Office.

The meeting had been called hastily the previous evening. Consequently it was not the normal fourteen-strong: "At least we've been spared the garrulous supernumeraries trying to justify their fees," reflected Glencorres as he watched the men around the table: Hamish Forbes of the National Scottish Bank, magnetised, like any wary banker, by the hint of trouble; George Nunnelly, Blenders' finance director, for whose ability and common sense he was always grateful; and the greying, rule-bound company secretary promoted beyond his limited abilities. The whisky barons present were the three most important of the seven whose fiefdoms made up the sinews of Blenders' commercial being – the other four were exercising the traditional boardroom privilege of visiting tropical markets during the seemingly endless Scottish winter.

Dougal Fordson was the centre of today's acrimony. Forceful and florid-faced, his obsessive ambition had pushed sales of 'Mountain Mist', an obscure brand which his accountant father had bought cheaply in the thirties, to No. 4 in the American market. Its success constituted his claim to succeed Glencorres as chairman, a claim the elderly peer resented for he found Fordson's instinctive vulgarity most objectionable: his one satisfaction in the morning's events lay in the knowledge that Fordson's ambitions now gave every promise of undoing him.

Beside him sat Andrew MacLintock, a lanky, amiable, good-natured athlete whose passion even now, in his mid-fifties, was still skiing. He treated his long-established, middle of the market brand 'White Heather' as a patrimony for which to be thankful, to be preserved and passed on intact.

He was Blenders' biggest shareholder, owning 10 per cent of the company, and Glencorres's own choice as successor, although the Earl had occasional reservations about the suitability of Andrew's forceful Eastern European wife, Marina.

Opposite Dougal Fordson sat Sir Luke Grey. Antipathy between these two was mutual and total. Tall, with chestnut hair and a World War I moustache, Luke was an open, but not a blatant, homosexual: his cheerfulness and wry description of his escapades for once justified the adjective 'gay'. He was conscientious in his work, promoted his malt 'Highland Dew' with panache and had made it a leader in its prestige market.

On this occasion the acrimony had flared when he said to Dougal, "It defeats me how you can have been so short-sighted. We all know currencies have been a nightmare since 1973 but a two-year contract fixed in dollars is crazy. Then on top of that to make it cut-price, without fixing an upper limit of what you will supply, just beggars belief.

"We've all agreed that it's not up to us to take long-term views on currencies. To argue on top of that that the dollar was going to be strong against the pound because everyone would want to hold dollars is naive rubbish. You don't have to be a currency expert to know that with a huge budget deficit, an election looming and half the Third World on the edge of bankruptcy, the Americans have no alternative but to print money as hard as they can, however loudly they protest to the contrary.

"All the time they have been manning the printing presses we have kept to our tight money policy here in Britain, so that American inflation is heading up while ours will be fairly stable. At the end of the day, the currency markets always acknowledge this, often with a bump. As I see it the rise in the pound to one dollar ninety since you signed that contract four months ago will mean that Blenders loses 25 cents on every bottle you ship. A little loss-leading to increase market share is all very well, but not when it bleeds the rest of us."

The silence of the others around the table signalled their support for this attack. Dougal, stung and by now redder in the face, retaliated with bluster.

"Bloody hell, you don't grow by sitting on your arse. I'm fed up with everybody saying we're just a bunch of order takers. I know we can make as good a deal in the States as some of the small independents have, but we've got to be ready to take risks. And this deal with Likkermart could be the biggest ever. All right some of Joseph Mabalian's business methods are not ones we would employ but he has made Likkermart the largest spirit discounter in the States: his companies have the trade sewn up in New York, Chicago and California. If he backs a brand it's made. When I met him in New York last summer he offered to promote 'Mountain Mist' ahead of any other brand if I gave him a two-year special price contract fixed in dollars. He said this gave the base for a major advertising campaign."

"And a fortune for himself," added Luke sharply.

"As Luke says, we do have a Group policy on currency," put in George Nunnelly.

Dougal flared, "I know you sent out a memo saying it should be policy to quote always in sterling and to avoid long-term commitments, but the only way I could get the deal was by quoting in dollars. Joseph said he wanted it that way so that his costs were fixed and I thought the dollar looked safe enough against the pound. After all, at the time I signed the deal the Swiss bankers were saying the pound looked overvalued."

"Usually a sure sign that it's cheap," Luke got in another jibe.

"Well, I don't understand the ins and outs of those things. But finally George, as group finance director, only recommends and it is my judgement and my brand. This deal with Likkermart could still make us the No. 1 seller in the States."

"And bankrupt Blenders in the process. George, have you worked out yet what Dougal's currency flutter is going to cost the rest of us?" Luke's brutal question was directed at Nunnelly.

"I can't say with any certainty. As far as I can see it's an open-ended commitment for the next two years. If the dollar just stays where it is, I could see us reporting a loss this year. If it weakens further, the loss will, of course, be greater."

Seizing gratefully on the opportunity, Glencorres intervened: "In that case we must make an announcement to the Stock Exchange at once. George, could you please draft it and, gentlemen, I suggest that we adjourn, then carry on after lunch."

When Andrew dutifully got back to Milo at Braithwaites later in the afternoon, he was uncharacteristically terse: "I can't say much on the telephone, old man: there's been a cock-up on currency and foreign sales. The money men are still trying to sort it out but it looks nasty. I'm coming down on the late afternoon plane. Look in for a drink after dinner and I'll fill you in as much as I can."

When told this, James commented resignedly: "It's better

than nothing, I suppose: it may keep the institutions happy for a day or so but we'll need something harder than that for them before long."

James's assessment of the institutions' reaction proved optimistic. Little else was going on in the market, which left the City's rumour factory free to produce the customary scare stories of widespread fraud and imminent bankruptcy. The 'bear' operators, who hope to make a profit by selling shares they may or may not own and buying them back cheaper – known as 'going short' – emerged in force: in spite of Braithwaites' reassurances the price fell a further 20p to end the day at 160p – a total fall of 70p from the 230p level before the announcement.

CHAPTER II

By the time Andrew reached his Lowndes Square flat that evening he was almost as exhausted from the hassle of Heathrow as the day's wrangling at Blenders and his worries about the future. He collapsed into a large armchair in the library and surveyed his surroundings gratefully. The treasures of three generations, Meissen figures, Empire enamel snuffboxes, Persian rugs, a Gainsborough and two Canalettos, reassured him. At least they would fetch enough at Christie's to keep his family for a few years.

He accepted with wordless thanks the tumbler of 'White Heather' and water Marina poured out. Her dark Slav elegance had worn well during the thirty years since, as a refugee from Tito, she'd married Andrew. Their marriage had been comfortable and singularly free from worry: now the long idyll was at risk.

"This damn foolery of Dougal's could wipe us out," said Andrew glumly. "The share price is collapsing and it looks as though there will be no dividend this year. The others can sit it out on their salaries: they're not borrowed to the hilt developing a ski-resort with a collapsing currency in the middle of a recession. God knows how we're going to meet the interest payments."

Bormona 2000 had originally been Marina's idea. A woman who combined style with a keener appetite for business than her husband, she had begun making money refurbishing old houses, then got drawn in to the world of property development. Some years previously, in the false dawn of the recovery from the first oil crisis, she had been offered a small share in a consortium formed to turn a remote Alpine valley on the French/Italian border into a total ski-resort, with hotels, flats, ski-school, swimming pools, saunas, even an interdenominational church.

The consortium wanted Andrew also, not for his modest business acumen, but for his prestige as a former captain of the Cambridge ski team and one-time Olympic racer. Andrew had accepted happily: "How nice to be paid for what one enjoys doing," he told his friends at White's. So he had not worried when one member of the consortium pulled out shortly afterwards. Andrew paid £500,000 to take over his share without much demur. The crisis had begun in the summer eight months previously when the main contractors, Wiplows, went dramatically bankrupt on a huge Middle-Eastern contract. With flats in Bormona pre-sold and hotel bookings taken for the winter, the consortium had been forced to hire an expensive French contractor, who demanded guarantees and a substantial cash advance. Marina, with a dangerous mix of Slav fatality and belief in her own flair, had urged Andrew to buy out the other shareholders, borrow the necessary £5 million and give the guarantees.

The money had proved difficult to raise but eventually Andrew had found a small merchant bank, Forde Jamieson, whose Chairman, Tim Weston, was prepared to take risks to expand the bank's business rapidly. He was also up for membership of White's and, although nothing was said openly, the interest Tim showed in the waiting list made it clear that he expected Andrew's support.

As security Andrew had pledged half his ten million Blenders' shares, then worth 250p each, giving a comfortable £12½ million backing to his £5 million loan, while the dividends helped to meet the interest charges. It was, he had explained to Tim, a short-term matter: repayment would begin with the sale of the first flats.

From that point the problems compounded horrifyingly.

There were difficulties with the foundations of the last apartment block and the French contractor fell further and further behind schedule. The jump in French inflation under the Socialists had sent the building costs rocketing, while many flats had been pre-sold at a price now showing a loss. Interest rates were rising everywhere and the charges on Andrew's borrowing already exceeded the dividends from his shares. Ominously, there had been a telephone call from Tim Weston the previous week suggesting a lunch at the bank, now due the next day.

"You realise," he said to Marina, "that if there is no Blenders dividend we face an interest bill of about £1 million a year. On top of that today's share price fall breaks a condition of the loan. I undertook that Forde's would have securities of ours of at least £10 million against the £5 million loan. At 160p the value of the 5 million shares which is our security is down to £8 million: they probably won't worry too much about that at the moment, but if the fall goes on, they could turn ugly. As it is, I am not exactly looking forward to tomorrow."

This gloomy summary of their affairs was broken by the arrival of the person to whom Andrew felt closest in the world (closer perhaps than to Marina, whose brain and energy sometimes made him uneasy), his daughter Sarah. Just twenty-two, she was tall, with the old-fashioned combination of large breasts and a tiny waist. Her eyes were alert and she combined an impulsive nature with a practical mind. Andrew doted on her: if she had not been sent away to Roedean, at Marina's firm behest, she would have become impossibly spoilt. As it was, she enjoyed her father's affection but did not trade on it.

"What have you been up to at Blenders?" she asked jokingly. "Will we have the little men in the bowler hats pounding on the door tomorrow saying they've come for the furniture? My friends from the brokers have been on the telephone all day: they're talking about nothing else. And I've told Leo that if he's ever going to get your stuffy old account, this is his chance." Sarah was personal assistant to Leo Hudson, of Leo Hudson Associates, a financial public relations firm. In the three years since Leo Hudson had emigrated from consumer promotion in Mayfair to corporate warfare in the City he had scored some spectacular wins in takeover struggles, using brasher techniques than the City was accustomed to. He had been the first to put the chairman of a company under takeover attack on to commercial television – this white-haired gentleman's appeal to the shareholders of his inefficient chainstore had been so effective that even the customers had declared they would shop elsewhere if the bid went through.

Leo Hudson's rivals said that he was pushy and unscrupulous, but lucky. The financial press, who preferred their public relations men to be ex-journalists down on their luck whom they could patronise, resented his glossy lifestyle. His clients sometimes worried about his unconventional tactics. But all respected his ability.

"At least I've got some good news," Sarah enthused. "Tim Weston called Leo today. Said they were thinking of us for the Forde Jamieson account and, guess what, that he'd like me to be part of the team working on it. I suppose it's because he knows you. Some day, perhaps, somebody will want me for me."

"I think," interspersed Marina firmly, "it's time we all had some dinner. Your father's had a hellish day and Milo is coming round to see him later."

"Amiable old Milo: what does he want? I suppose father's version of today's drama so that Braithwaites have something to say to their clients on the telephone tomorrow. Still, I'd better be nice to him: Braithwaites are very influential and could help me on the Weston job – they're still a bit standoffish about Tim. And having James Murray as a godfather shouldn't do me any harm in that direction either."

But when Milo arrived he looked uncharacteristically serious and Andrew took him off to his study almost at once. After Andrew had recounted the Board meeting, Milo looked even more sombre. "Isn't there any way out of the contract with Mabalian?" he asked.

"It's a pretty straightforward one and Mabalian's lawyers have made it as watertight as they know how. I suppose we could always say that the dollar crisis constituted force majeure and employ even more expensive lawyers. But that's not our way of doing business. I think we'd rather put in a loss for the year than do that."

"There's nothing there to help the share price," said Milo gloomily, "the bears have been going short and we want to come in and support you but I don't see that we can. It's terribly embarrassing for us with clients sitting on huge lines of stock bought at much higher prices. We shall have to put on our best 'It'll be all right in the long term' act to try to discourage the sellers and hope to limit the fall."

Then realising that the evening's backgammon would be underway shortly at the Turf Club, he declined a second brandy and left, reflecting that his relative looked more miserable than even Blenders' problems would warrant.

As Milo was saying, "Evening Fred," to the Turf Club's porter seated in his glass and mahogany cubicle, Luke Grey emerged from his Berkeley Square flat to walk to another club, Nelson's, an establishment off Bond Street he frequented in the equal certainty of congenial company. As he passed his astrakhan-collared coat to the young man dressed as a nineteenth-century sailor, who kept a wary watch on all arrivals, he felt tired but far from miserable.

He had never understood the absence of an English word for that state of mind the Germans call *Schadenfreude*. It was not after all an exclusively German characteristic: at that point he was actively rejoicing in Dougal's discomfiture. "It'll hit the value of my shares," he reflected, "but I'm not going to sell them. They'll recover in a couple of years and if it cuts that vulgarian down to size it will be well worth it."

"Evening, darling. Fancy something?" Paul, the fresh-faced barman appeared to have been sewn into his midshipman's outfit.

"Only a whisky sour."

"Got to do something for the profits of that company of yours, I suppose. You'll have had a heavy day, too, from what the papers say," he garruled on. "Never mind, dear, there's a nice theatrical number down at the other end of the bar who's new to me but looks just your type."

Peering through the three-quarter light, Luke saw something he indeed fancied – a young man with fair hair, open features, slim hips, decked in nonchalant Piero di Monzi elegance.

"She's been fighting the old men off all evening," said Paul, "but she might let you buy her a drink."

Which the young man, who gave his name as Robin Jones, did. He had, he said, just left RADA. No, he didn't come here often; it was a bit grand for him. He'd had a date, but his friend hadn't shown up and probably wasn't coming now.

As they talked, desire stirred in Luke.

"Like to dance a little?" he asked.

"If you would."

The floor, lit intermittently by psychedelic strobes, was not yet crowded, but in the alcoves hopeful eyes scanned each new arrival. Robin danced lithely and easily to the heavy funk with its raw insistent beat; almost casually he brushed his groin against Luke, who felt desire enflame.

"Would you like a nightcap with me? I live near here," he suggested as they left the floor.

"Why not?" replied Robin simply.

CHAPTER III

"Blenders' blunder," alliterated the *Daily News* headline the next morning while the Lux column in the *Financial Times* took waspish pleasure in the company's discomfiture: "Blenders has never been forthcoming with information on its activities: the one hint it has given in recent months was that much should be expected from America. Instead things have gone badly awry and the suddenness of yesterday's debacle suggests that the traditional reticence may be due to the Board being as much in the dark as shareholders. Now the inability to quantify the loss on the 'Mountain Mist' contract raises the fear that it could prove open-ended. Until this and the dividend position are clearer, the share price faces the problem of finding a proper level."

"Good stuff," said Tim Weston cheerfully reading the passage aloud to his junior partner, Frank Higgins, in his newly-panelled chairman's room in Forde Jamieson's London Wall skyscraper offices. "Just what we want. It destroys the Board's credibility: makes things easier for us."

"What do you mean 'for us'? We have nothing to do with Blenders."

"Not at the moment perhaps: but think about it." Tim spoke with unusual intensity. "Blenders could be our big chance. If you look at our growth pattern, we began by taking over small companies, then progressed to medium and larger ones. Now we are ready for the really big one – all the readier in that no one is expecting us to do anything at all at the moment."

The growth in Tim Weston's business, from the backwaters of investment counselling little more than a decade previously to control of Forde Jamieson, a small but old-established merchant bank, had made him a folk hero to the financial press and the small investor. But the Establishment viewed him with an uneasy mixture of suspicion and respect, uncertain whether to assimilate or reject him.

They could forgive his suburban origins, which indeed had their value, for they enabled him to attract the bright and ambitious who felt stifled by the obstinate survival of family and connections in the promotion pattern of Establishment firms. The problem lay more in the City's inability to classify the new Forde Jamieson, for it failed to fit any of the neat traditional categories, being part bank, part investment company with a finger in many industries, a major property developer, and the owner of two highly successful store chains – Kalorykount, the pioneers of takeaway slimming meals, and Slimfit, biggest and trendiest in the selling of jeans and casual wear. "Can you fit a Slimfit?" asked the posters in Kalorykount threateningly. "Too tight? Try Kalorykount" riposted the placards in Slimfit. Tim called it integration; the City's older and warier inhabitants called it gimmickry.

There was still some vagueness about his early business manoeuvrings. They had not been substantial enough at the time to attract much attention and success, when it came, arrived in such a landslide as to make them irrelevant. The City knows that commercial empires are seldom built by strict adherence to the spirit of the law and even the most respectable secretly admire those who once cut their corners fine – provided it paid and went undetected.

The few who had bothered to delve reported that Weston's early tactics were just about legal at the time – and had proved highly profitable both to him and his clients. Instead of the normal spread of successful companies he had used his clients' funds to build up large holdings in two small companies with poor profits, a low share price – and substantial properties still in the books at very out-of-date values. If the malicious are to be believed, he had first bought blocks of shares for himself, financed by a bank manager who were also cut in for a share of the profits. They were large, for an alliance with a property developer enabled him to mount highly rewarding takeover bids for the companies.

The sale of the properties provided the financial ammunition for the next bids, a leap-frogging procedure which, shrewdly timed and executed, had continued up to 1973 by which time Tim Weston was established as the country's favourite grammar-school tycoon, the man with no connections who had nevertheless carved out a City empire. The success of these early takeovers had pushed his share price to dizzy heights which enabled him to acquire first Forde Jamieson, a rundown merchant bank with an historic name, then Gem Assurance, a sleepy but cash-rich insurance company with premiums flowing in steadily for investment in whatever Weston thought right.

At the same time the glamour of his accomplishment swelled the original posse of investment clients to an army, marshalled now into neat formations of unit trusts. Each was dedicated ostensibly to a different aim – income, capital growth, technology, overseas – but the holders were united in their belief that association with Tim Weston made them kin, if not to Midas, at least to John D. Rockefeller.

Their faith had been tested on occasion but had been amply rewarded. Their mentor had anticipated the financial crisis of 1974–76, and profited from it. Properties had been sold at the height of the boom and loans paid off while others were still borrowing their way to disaster. He bought gold when it was neglected then sold it at a threefold profit to the Swiss as they panicked their Arab clients into it. When share prices collapsed in 1974 after the oil price rise, he bought heavily – and sold a year later when prices rushed up in relief that the system had survived, before the sober realisation set in that it would never be quite the same again.

Outside business his life was featureless. He had married his secretary, who ran his house and brought up his two children with the same efficiency she had shown in his office. He lived in comfort, but not in style, and while he could always be relied on to take advertising space in charity programmes, played little part in fashionable life.

Now, at forty–two, he was contemplating the biggest move in his career. Ambitious excitement gripped him: "Blenders has always fascinated me; it's the one really vulnerable company in the top thirty. When you study it you see that it is no more than a loose federation of family firms – but the business they are in is one of the best in Britain. To sell most British goods in world markets we have had, over the longer term, to make them progressively cheaper by devaluing the currency – there's no other way to persuade buyers to tolerate poor workmanship and unreliable deliveries. What prestige abroad is there in owning a British Leyland car? Where is there a factory manager who boasts of his Alfred Herbert machine tools?

"But Scotch is something quite different: it's the only whisky that people want to have in their bar or admit to drinking. Scotch sells itself – and would still sell if the £ went back to $2.80.

"But this very sellers' market has made Blenders flabby: the Directors live like lairds and most of the salesmen are no more than order takers. Every one of those brands is a jealously guarded empire and they spend half their time trying to score off one another.

"The profit record is respectable enough in a stodgy way and they have plenty of cash. But with a product like that and selling worldwide they should have a record in the IBM class."

"What about the American deal which has gone sour?"

"Our New York office sent this on the Rapifax last night

– the London market is bound to get hold of it today. That should shake out some sellers and I want us to buy their stock." Tim passed over to Frank a page taken from the Wall Street Reprint, a publication unique to that citadel of capitalism and one of those beautifully simple ideas which makes its originator rich for life without the need for further innovative thought. It reprints for the public at large the research on companies produced by brokers for their institutional clients – and charges a stiff price for this mix of intelligence and self-advertisement.

A breezy report from a Chicago broker was headed: "Earnings leap for Likkermart. A two-year supply contract with the producers of 'Mountain Mist' fixed in dollars last year will enable the Chicago-listed liquor discounter to gain market share strongly *and* improve margins. Since the contract signing, the $ has slumped by 20% and competing Scotch brands are hoisting their US prices to hold margins. But Likkermart's fixed price dollar contract will allow it to undercut the competition, market aggressively and still show a handsome margin.

"Likkermart's break spells problems for brand-owners Blenders. How long can it afford to supply whisky at a price below current costs? Blenders has been a favoured stock with Scotch-loving investors. Now is the moment to sell, and buy Likkermart – the stock which will gain from Blenders' losses."

"I wonder what the contract will cost them in the end," mused Frank.

"I doubt whether they know themselves. It certainly won't break them and a new management would be in a very strong position. It could argue the legality of the contract, plead force majeure on the currency, or, if things got really bad, put 'Mountain Mist' into liquidation and let Likkermart argue it out with the receiver."

"How big are Blenders?"

"There are 100 million shares in issue, so at 160p they're worth £160 million."

"Much the same size as we are. It doesn't leave much scope for generosity or knockout bids. What could be squeezed out of it?"

"Frank," reiterated Tim persuasively, by now in the grip of his own plans, "Blenders is a gold mine. Scotch is almost the only world monopoly that we have left in this country and it is just that which has made the company fat and overstaffed. Knock all those marketing companies together and you could slash overheads. Do you know, each of the seven main brands has representative offices in New York supporting seven separate staffs? As far as I can see their principal activity is to outspend each other's promotional budgets. Have one office, charge what the market will bear and the profits will double, if not treble." Impelled by an excess of energy, Tim began to pace up and down the room.

"It's the last great unconsummated merger in British industry. It fascinates me. I have been working on it from different angles for some time now, waiting for an opportunity. This could be it. We must go into the market and start building up holdings. But obviously don't let any one account get more than 4.9% of the company which would mean announcing our purchases officially. In addition, I am working on the possibility of getting big blocks direct . . ."

"You mean Andrew MacLintock?"

A wry nod. "Among others. He's coming in to lunch today. It really is remarkably fortuitous. Please join us, Frank, and, meanwhile, will you have a word with the investment department?"

The request sounded innocuous enough but Frank knew it for the challenge it was. Merchant banks with investment departments are expected to keep them rigorously separated from company acquisition activities: in theory it is obligatory that the right hand should not know what the left hand is doing. In practice it can be crucial to enter a bid with a substantial block of shares already in friendly hands but even in as opportunistic a bank as Forde Jamieson, the pressure can never be overt. The fund managers have the freedom to say "No", for they have the final responsibility.

Frank felt ready, even anxious, for this chance to prove himself. He was still relatively young – in his early thirties – consciously classless, and beginning to cultivate the finer pleasures: some of his earlier share dealing gains had been swiftly reinvested in fine Victorian water colours chosen by himself. Hair unfashionably short and with a square almost Prussian face, he was handsome in a solid way, the heaviness lightened by the intensity of his nervous energy. So far that energy had been applied to his business life, pushing him through the London School of Economics and the Harvard Business School with speed and distinction, then swiftly up McKinsey's corporate ladder, finally driving him out of the restrictive security of the salariat into the more testing world of the corporate battlefield. He was still unmarried – his sexual appetites were conventional but had found no strong attachment: the bed in his mews house behind Grosvenor Square was shared by a succession of "models" and small-part television actresses, decorative, sexually talented and emotionally shallow.

He had joined Tim Weston three years previously to rationalise a string of industrial companies and subsequently had been involved in the acquisition of Gem Assurance. Command of the Blenders' operation represented a major chance inside Forde Jamieson's loosely structured hierarchy. If Blenders were the company's big opportunity, even more so was it his.

In spite of Tim Weston's intellectual ascendancy, the unit trust managers were far from automatons, as Frank reflected uneasily in the lift to the investment department. They, too, were ambitious and in the performance of their trusts lay their passport to advancement.

Those who had dragged their feet at the time of Tim's most recent enthusiasm had been spared an expensive involvement in a failed takeover and subsequently, in a guarded way, praised for their shrewd far-sightedness. This example, Frank was uncomfortably aware, was going to make his present task that much harder.

His first target was the chief dealer, Len: large, florid, with a quick mind, the clipped speech characteristic of his trade and a sharp appetite for brokers' lunches. "What's going on in Blenders?" Frank opened.

"Some big selling. The market's got hold of a very bearish piece in that Wall Street Reprint. Jim Macdonald is thinking of selling a hundred thousand – just asked me to get the price."

"Let me have a word with him before you deal. There may be other fish to fry here."

Jim Macdonald ranked as the most independent-minded of the department's managers. Trained in the rigorous school of the Scottish investment trusts, his addiction to basic principles and his successful side-stepping of Tim Weston's last manoeuvre had enhanced both the performance of his trusts and his reputation in the department. If he were a seller, it would be uphill work to persuade the others to buy Blenders. Frank summoned up his energy as he strolled over to Jim's desk; the stocky Scotsman radiated intellectual aggression, lightly concealed behind the jocular tone of his opening shot: "Well, Frank, and what do you want us to stuff the trusts with today?"

"I am more concerned, Jim, that you will in fact be able to buy your Blenders back lower down," Frank stonewalled guardedly.

"I should never have bought them in the first place," countered Jim. "One of the basic rules of investment taught in Edinburgh is never to invest in Scottish companies. The Scots must emigrate to be successful. It's a good rule that, and I made a great mistake when I let a London broker persuade me to break it. But it's a mistake I'm just about to correct."

Forde Jamieson paid lip service to the division between the bank's own business and the investment activities of the unit trusts. Frank saw he was going to have to blur that line to win the Scotsman's co-operation.

"Sell by all means, Jim; it'll scare a few holders and get the price down. But when it's down, I believe you should buy back twice what you sold. Blenders' independence may not last forever."

"Who's going to bid for them with that crazy contract around their necks?"

There is a time for indiscretion, Frank realised.

"Could be us."

"Us? Don't be crazy. Even at 160p Blenders is worth £160 million in the stock market. With our shares at 90p we are valued at £180 million."

"Provided we can get our own shares underwritten we could do it; in one move we would have doubled our size."

"And if Blenders is the can of worms it looks like, given ourselves a problem which might bring us down?"

"I don't believe their problems are as serious as that," said Frank with a confidence he did not altogether feel.

"You check that carefully," riposted Jim. "It won't do anything for my unit holders' confidence if the parent company gets into trouble: the last thing I want is a string of holders selling their units back. Still, if the idea gets around that we're interested, that would be enough to put the price better so I'll cancel the order and instead buy some if they fall 10p or so. But I'll expect you to keep me in touch."

This first major hurdle negotiated, Frank strolled around the department going through the ritual hints and verbal semaphoring long established in Forde Jamiesons as indicating interest in a takeover target. Fund managers did not have to take the hint, but to ignore too many hints from above could prove damaging in the long run to performance – and therefore promotion prospects – unless redeemed by a remarkable success in the market. There being, as Tim Weston was fond of observing, no substitute for inside information, such success was not easy to achieve unaided.

Frank found his audience receptive enough to report back to Tim that accumulation would begin as soon as the first shake-out looked to be over.

CHAPTER IV

The business day starts at Braithwaites with a 9.15 meeting. It covers the financial news in the morning papers, discusses the company results expected that day, weighs up market rumours and decides tactics.

James, whose turn it was to take the meeting, was struggling to appear alert. *Rigoletto* the previous night had been unduly late finishing. He could never understand why Covent Garden favoured three long intervals – perhaps bar profits were the balancing item in its notoriously stretched budget. Clarissa, whose energy was more nocturnal than his, had then decided she was hungry and wanted late supper in the Garrick where they met friends and, inevitably, stayed on drinking Beaumes de Venise until one o'clock. He had reached the age when over-indulgence kept him awake and he had slept poorly. Perhaps made more perceptive – or imaginative – by this he had the impression that the young eyes of the assembled investment analysts and salesmen appeared more critical and ambitious than usual.

Summoning his thoughts, James opened, "The main topic today, of course, is Blenders. The papers seem pretty hostile and I can't say I blame them altogether – Blenders have always been too complacent about the press. But I'm afraid it doesn't make our life any easier. Now, Milo, what's the news from Andrew yesterday evening?"

"Not too good I'm afraid. The worrying thing is that no one on the Board had any idea that things were so far adrift. It was only when George Nunnelly, their finance director, queried some of the figures in the 'Mountain Mist' budget that the whole thing came out. George has the right ideas but he doesn't carry enough weight."

"Emma," James spoke to his plump and pretty secretary, "make a note that we should get Lord Glencorres in to lunch. We must exert a little pressure on him to turn these individualists of his into something approaching a twentieth-century corporation." Turning back to Milo, "How serious is the damage?"

"No one knows. It depends on how much Likkermart orders and how the currency moves. If you're pessimistic, instead of last year's £40 million profit there could be a small loss: if the dollar falls further, then of course the loss will be greater. The good news is that the contract runs only to the autumn of next year and the National Scottish Bank have said they'll see the company through."

"That's something at least. What have they got in the way of assets?"

"Stocks of whisky in bond are worth about 300p a share at the moment."

"Hmm. Enough to tempt a takeover bidder, but not enough to support the share price, which makes our position a bit tricky. Not only are we brokers to the company, so that we can't easily ditch them by turning sellers, but most of our clients bought Blenders' shares at higher prices. Even though the price is probably too high, in fact decidedly toppy, I think we shall have to take the no-man's-land line – too late to sell, too early to buy."

Some other broking houses, without these constraints, were taking a more decisive view. Around the City the automatic dialling machines whirred: heads were lowered into telephones and the voices spoke with quiet urgency, the confidentiality increased by a hand cupped around the mouthpiece:

". . . Blenders can't work out the size of the problem."

". . . the first loss is usually the smallest. We'd cut them now."

". . . the chart looks dreadful."

". . . the Americans are bound to come in as sellers on that piece in the Wall Street Reprint."

". . . let a few go. There'll be a chance to buy them back lower down."

". . . it was right to sell them yesterday, and it's still right today."

". . . if you want to get some away, do it now."

Tim Weston smiled happily as the television screen showed the price ebbing steadily to 150p. He asked Frank: "What do the brokers say?"

"Braithwaites are doing their best bedside act inviting people to hang on, saying everything will be all right in the long run. But they haven't got much of a case. Some of the other houses, though, are strong sellers."

"Good. Let's start buying at 140p; there's no point in being too greedy."

Pre-lunch drinks at White's were proving tricky for Andrew. Some of those he talked to pointedly avoided the topic of Blenders: others were divided between the sympathetic and the few who openly asked, "What shall we do with our Blenders' shares?"

"I'm hanging on to mine," was Andrew's invariable reply, reflecting to himself, "as they're pledged to Forde Jamieson anyhow I haven't much option." He was due there at one o'clock and, although apprehensive at the prospect, for once was grateful to quit the congenial bar early.

* * *

Lunch at Forde Jamieson is a carefully designed blend of the traditional and the functional: the oak panelling and the butler are balanced by Nouvelle Cuisine, while mineral water is served with the same assiduity as the excellent wines. And although the bank does not emulate one of its Teutonic rivals which, when it realised that lunch was one of the main business activities of the day, put its executives' digestions at risk by instituting a double shift, little time is wasted on discussion of current television, sport or the condition of Home Counties' gardens.

Only three people were to lunch with Andrew: Tim Weston, Frank Higgins and the manager of the banking department.

"I know we mustn't pry too deeply," said Tim, using the traditional City lead-in for a series of direct questions, "but it would be fascinating to know a little more of what lay behind that very terse statement of Blenders' yesterday which, if I may say so, raised rather more questions than it answered. As we are holding Blenders' shares as collateral for what, by our standards, is a very large loan, we have, I believe, a legitimate interest. At the same time I hear from France that things are going far from smoothly on your Bormona development. If everything were to go wrong simultaneously, it could put us all in a most awkward situation."

Amateur businessman that he was, Andrew knew well that "a most awkward situation" was a clear reference to the fact that not only did the collateral no longer cover his loan adequately but that his banker was afraid that it might shrink even further.

Tim continued, "And if something has gone irretrievably astray at Blenders, I hate to think of the possible consequences."

"So do I," echoed Andrew to himself, while replying aloud with one of Marina's favourite Hapsburg aphorisms, "As I see it, the situation is desperate, but not serious. This year's profits are a write-off and probably next year's too, but that's all. There is no long-term threat to Blenders' future. The trouble is just in one subsidiary which made a lunatic two-year supply contract to an American distributor, fixed in dollars, last summer. The fall in the dollar since then means that every bottle we sell costs us money now. As the wretched American will be able to undersell the competition using an established brand, you can be certain he will call for every bottle we can produce."

"What scope is there for delaying deliveries – it happens often enough on profitable contracts?" asked Frank.

"He can sue if he doesn't get certain minimum quantities," said Andrew ruefully, "and I am told this morning that those minimum quantities would put us into loss this year just on the basis of the present exchange rate. Unless the $ recovers and there's precious little sign of that, the loss will be at least as bad next year. In my book, that makes things desperate."

"Why should they not be serious too?" asked Tim.

"Because of the two-year limit on the problem and because our bankers have indicated that they will support us through it. We have, after all, been doing business with them in one form or another for over a hundred years."

"Have you thought of putting the offending subsidiary into liquidation?" – a pointed question from Frank.

"To be honest, we haven't. Now that you bring it up, it is, I suppose, technically possible. And I know that anything is thinkable since Rolls Royce was let go, but that's not our style. I think we're too proud."

"So long as you can afford to be, that's fine," said Tim suavely.

By this time the coffee – strong black espresso – was being served and Tim deftly steered the talk around to Andrew's own predicament.

"From what you say, it doesn't sound as though there is likely to be much in the way of a dividend next year either," mused Tim. "I don't see any bank letting a company pay more than a token amount in the circumstances."

Andrew nodded a glum agreement.

"How will this affect the servicing of your loan: at current interest rates it's costing about £1 million a year?" The stomach-turning question was out in the open. "On top of that, the way things are going, or rather not going, in France, I take it there's little chance of the capital repayments you hoped to make this year."

More mute, miserable agreement from Andrew.

"The worrying thing from our point of view," continued Tim relentlessly, "is that the fall in the share price brings the cover for your £5 million loan below the £10 million we had agreed – at 150p, where the shares stood at noon, the five million shares are worth £7½ million. Can you put in any more collateral – I believe you hold another five million Blenders' in your own name?"

"I am not sure whether I am in a position to pledge them also. Having given a personal guarantee to the French contractors, I must keep some assets free. Quite honestly, if it were not for that wretched personal guarantee, I would be happier to cut my losses on the whole business. The problems at Blenders rather rule out expensive personal ventures just now."

This was the moment for Tim gradually to put on the pressure.

"Quite. Tell me, what's your own estimate of the very worst that finishing Bormona could cost?"

"Another £5 million at the very, very worst."

"Well, let's see. Still taking the gloomy view, namely that French delays prevent you making any repayments over the next two years and that interest rates continue at their present levels, then rolling up the interest charges could bring your total borrowing requirement to something like £15 million. At today's share price of 150p your ten million Blenders' shares are worth £15 million. But what you have told me of the American contract and the dividend outlook makes that price look toppy to me. You probably saw the Lux comment in the *Financial Times* this morning."

Andrew well remembered the barbed conciseness.

"In a bear market," continued Tim, "I could see the shares down to 100p – which would mean borrowings of £15 million against security of £10 million. You don't need me to tell you that that's not a banking proposition."

Sensing a lifeline, Andrew asked tentatively, "Might it be a proposition of some other sort?"

"Let us look at the alternatives. You could, in theory, sell your ten million shares on the market now, raising enough money to repay us and finish Bormona."

"But that would also finish me as a Board member. And there would be the most frightful hue and cry in the financial press: I can just see the *Daily News* headline – "Blenders' Director Goes Liquid" – on top of that it would leave me with Bormona as my only asset. All in all, I would rather consider almost anything else."

Tim's manner became almost unctuous: "I should like to be able to help you. In my judgement the problems at both Bormona and Blenders are essentially short-term. They are not in any way connected and it's just bad luck for you that they happened to occur at the same time. Now, I have also been doing some work on Blenders' underlying value. The stocks alone, net of borrowing, must be worth well over £3 a share. And the goodwill value of some of the best-known names in the whisky trade are worth a pound or two. All in all, the shares have an underlying worth of, at the very least, 350p.

"Here's my proposition. I'll take a risk if you will. The bank will lend you the £15 million at current interest rates on the security of your ten million shares; in the long run, I reckon, those shares will be worth over £30 million. The risk I ask you to take is that you give me an option to buy your shares in Blenders at 250p, nearly twice today's price. Obviously, it would not do for a director to sell his shares at a higher price than other shareholders could get in the market, so my option would only become operative if the market price stayed above 250p for three days."

To Andrew the offer appeared slightly quixotic. It may be, he thought, that Tim believes I will become chairman of Blenders in due course and that I could then steer the Blenders' banking business his way. Which, I suppose, would be fair enough.

Out loud he replied, "I think that's a very handsome offer. There's only one condition I feel I must make: that the option be good for my lifetime only. I don't feel I should bind my heirs and successors in this way, so in the circumstances I ought to take out short-term life assurance to cover the borrowing. Can you arrange that?"

As Tim's plans involved speedy action on the Blenders front, and Andrew looked fit enough, he decided not to quibble. "That doesn't seem unreasonable. Frank, could you get all the papers drawn up this afternoon, please."

"Why not bring them around this evening, Frank, join us for dinner and I'll sign them then."

Andrew had remembered Sarah's new assignment to work on the Forde Jamieson account and thought it could help her to meet Frank, whose straightforwardness he found appealing.

CHAPTER V

Frank arrived in Lowndes Square punctually at eight. The careless, slightly worn opulence of Andrew's high-ceilinged flat contrasted sharply with the predictably toning, decorator chic in which Frank's newly moneyed friends lived, inspired usually by the more luxurious hotels to which their expense accounts gave them access. In Andrew's case the inspiration, and often the source, was the family house in Lammermuir from which had come the oil painting of an earlier MacLintock in the uniform of a Colonel in Wellington's army, dominating the hall as he had once his regiment, a Louis Seize chair and a deeply polished bureau concealing the slight fraying on one side of a Persian runner. In the drawing room, lit by standard lamps and a number of deep-fringed, silk-shaded Chinese vases on low tables, eighteenth- and nineteenth-century English and French furniture co-existed in a happy alliance to which some of Marina's icons added a dash of Balkan exoticism.

Marina greeted Frank with warm interest: bankers held for her the glamour which actors did for many of her contemporaries, and she had already marked down Frank as a future star. But while Frank fascinated her, he found his attention held by Sarah, as she apologised for her father who was in the study telephoning the French contractors.

From her mother she had inherited highish cheekbones and a skin which looked always as though it had recently been in the sun, from her father an athletic frame and thick chestnut hair. The two elegantly-dressed women, Marina a little more heavily-built and with the face of one of her icon Madonnas, were a high-spirited, attractive and formidable pair. God, they're magnificent, thought Frank, strong personalities, but nothing mannish about them.

Marina, like Frank's colleagues, did not believe in wasting time on pleasantries. "How lovely to meet someone from Forde Jamieson's at last. Apart from the fact that Tim Weston has had the imagination to back our unusual development, I have been a great admirer of his for years. Now tell me, how long does he think we're going to have to put up with these ruinous interest rates? They are doing dreadful damage to some of my friends in property."

"They are a nasty hazard in that world." Frank didn't believe in showing more of his hand than he had to.

"Yes," said Marina, whose obstinacy was tactful, "but you must work on some assumption as to whether they are going up or down."

"Until American rates ease, which does not look very likely in the short-term, I don't see that ours can fall much."

"You bankers needn't worry, of course, sitting there earning a fortune on your loans, but it's difficult for anyone who is actually doing anything. Still, Sarah tells me Leo Hudson's have to improve your image, so I suppose excess profits are as good a place as any to start."

Frank was enjoying the gentle verbal sparring: "Windfall gains from the Government's monetary policy have to be explained away by every bank. Our problem is a bit more specific. Because we are a new group which has taken control of an old bank people must feel confident that we are sound and don't take silly risks. On top of that, we are bound to get involved in a takeover or two, and we want to make sure that the Hudson outfit is with us and not with the opposition."

Andrew entered, a glass of 'White Heather' in his hand, and greeted Frank in a friendly way. "At long last those

Frog contractors are making progress in Bormona – it is about time we had some good news."

"All we need now is for someone to make a takeover bid for Blenders," chipped in Sarah brightly, "then we'd get a lovely price for our shares and wouldn't have to worry where the next ski-lift was coming from."

"And have Leo Hudson mastermind the defence. I don't think Glencorres would much relish going on the box," countered her father.

Frank, sensing danger, swiftly steered the conversation back to the Alps. "I'm glad to hear things are moving at Bormona. Tell me, Andrew, just how good is the skiing there?"

"Quite honestly, it's incredible. Sunny nursery slopes by the hotels and glorious powder runs from the peak, some easy, some where even a guide has to mind his eye. And on the Mont Verre glacier there's marvellous Spring skiing until the end of June. I can't understand why the whole place wasn't developed years ago: it knocks Val d'Isère into a cocked hat. Sarah, who has skied everywhere, including the Andes, says there's nowhere she'd rather go."

When father and daughter discovered that Frank, though a late starter, was both a keen and competent skier who never missed a winter on the slopes, they warmed perceptibly to him and moved into dinner deep in discussion of runs they knew, the hazards and joys of powder snow, the merits of various types of skis, and the other aspects of the most exhilarating of sports.

After the main course, Lammermuir venison, accompanied by Marina's Balkan red cabbage and a 1966 bottle from the second growth Bordeaux vineyard Blenders had bought when both diversification and European expansion were fashionable, Frank turned to Sarah: "We mustn't indulge ourselves in skiing chat all evening: tell me why everyone says Leo Hudson is so good and what you think makes him so successful."

"Obviously I'm prejudiced, because I like him, but I'm

sure the answer is because he's got great style and a quick mind. Other PR men wait outside the boardroom and do their best with the brief that's given them, but where there's a takeover Leo insists on sitting in on the meeting.

"Bankers are good at getting figures right but many bids involve more than just money and bankers can often be hopeless about the human side and not alienating people. That's where Leo is so good – and he can understand the figures as well. But isn't our brief a general one to make the City think Forde Jamieson is a respectable set-up rather than to get involved in specific bids?"

"Yes, of course." Again, Frank veered away from the dangerous topic, aware that he was getting on to treacherous ground with a woman whom he found powerfully attractive. A spasm of self-loathing was triggered by the realisation that double-dealing with this friendly, open family might kill any chance of discovering whether the attraction could ripen and be mutual.

He turned to Andrew: "What's Blenders going to do about Dougal Fordson? He's landed you in this mess: surely he can't be allowed to stay on?"

"It's not, as I am sure you know, quite as simple as that. We could relieve him of executive responsibilities, but only the shareholders can sack him from the Board. He's aggressive, and the company is his whole life. I think we have enough on our hands without public boardroom rows and noisy shareholders' meetings. It may come up at tomorrow's board, but I doubt if anything will be done. However, I have to catch up with my sleep, so, Frank, let's now go through these documents you've brought."

Later, as Frank was leaving, Andrew said: "Sarah and I plan to go over to Bormona at the end of next week to see if those contractors are really doing as well as they say. Now that the Bank has such an interest, maybe you would like to come with us?"

The reply was completely sincere: "I can think of nothing I should like better." Turning to Sarah, "Let's have some lunch tomorrow if you're free. We could fix travelling times then – and talk enough about Leo Hudson's to justify the outing. I'll call you in the morning."

Chapter VI

Some hours after Andrew had gone to bed in London, two men had a morning meeting in the Tokyo office of another whisky company, Sonkay Spirits. Where the mahogany elegance of Blenders' Adam building asserts the company's claim to share in Scotland's history and tradition, Sonkay's glass-sheathed tower affirms its rank as a leading state in the expanding empire of Japan Inc. The cosmopolitan modern decor hints at the inhabitant's identity only through carefully hung and lit scrolls of traditional saké brewing.

In the twentieth-storey office of the chief executive, Mr Nobutaka Seizo sat on a low sofa beneath an expensive Picasso visual joke in which bottles are distorted into a suggestive anatomical illusion, talking to his old university colleague, Mr Yasuko Watanabe, head of the Japanese investment house, Monawa. Monawa is another vital element in Japan Inc, a giant international stockbroker with offices in every established financial centre and in many cities which only aspire to this status. Monawa's profits number it among Japan's top one hundred corporations and its power in the markets is legendary. The combined force of its batteries of salesmen can move the price of even the largest company by 20 per cent in a day, a power which is sparingly used but both respected and feared.

After the obligatory mutual enquiries and compliments on family, health and golf, protocol permitted Mr Seizo to broach the reasons for the meeting.

"It is kind of you to come and see me and to take an interest in the affairs of the company."

"My company values its relationship with your great business." Mr Watanabe was determined not to let any of Monawa's rivals be involved in Sonkay's next issue of shares.

"I mentioned to you that we are concerned about the problems which we hear are affecting our Scottish friends at Blenders as a result of their unfortunate contract with Likkermart. I should value your opinion as to how serious these problems are."

"They have said they will make a loss this year. From our office in London I learn it is feared that they will make a loss next year also. It is a great misfortune."

"You are aware, of course, that they supply us with the malt whisky we blend into our leading brand, 'Imperial'. Many of the other Scottish whisky distillers are angry about this. They say it encourages competition from Japan and that Blenders should not sell to us. If I were a Scottish distiller I do not believe I would supply my competitors with essential ingredients but fortunately for Sonkay, when there was an over-supply of malt after the first oil crisis, Blenders made a seven-year agreement with us. That agreement ends this year and it is of great importance to us that it should be renewed. The problems in America make it almost certain that they will renew, as we could help their finances with advance payments. But we are very concerned in case Blenders' weakness should lead to a change of control which could affect a new contract."

Mr Seizo paused to allow Mr Watanabe to respond: "Our London office say there has been much activity in the shares and many rumours. But there is nothing definite."

"My colleagues and I have had lengthy discussions about our Scottish friends' difficulties. How would it be regarded if we were to buy their shares as a way of keeping off intruders? Naturally we would inform their Board."

Two slim, kimono-clad girls brought in small, fragile

bowls of fresh tea, giving Mr Watanabe time to consider this startling proposal.

"No Japanese company has ever become involved in a takeover battle on a foreign stock exchange. Do we not believe ourselves that the control of a great enterprise is too important an issue to be decided just by the shareholders?"

"In Japan that is true," agreed Mr Seizo, "but when we are dealing with 'gaijin', should we not do as the 'gaijin' does?"

"If you decide to do that," – Mr Watanabe was now tacitly assenting to the proposal – "then it would be better to say nothing to the Board of Blenders until you have bought 5 per cent of the company, when the British regulations force you to make a public announcement. If you tell them before you begin they might act dishonourably by buying shares for themselves, or they might even make announcements and start political difficulties. But when you have your 5 per cent you can tell them you are acting in order to preserve their independence and their Board will then almost certainly support you. It would not be advisable for a Japanese company to attempt to buy Blenders completely, but you are allowed to own up to 29.9 per cent without having to make an offer to buy out the other shareholders. And with 29.9 per cent you could prevent anyone else buying the company – and naturally also you could expect to be represented on the Board and to influence the policy."

"That would be most satisfactory for my company. Now I must report our discussion to my colleagues."

Early that afternoon Mr Watanabe received from Sonkay's investment department an order to buy up to 5 per cent of Blenders' shares.

Monawa's London office in Throgmorton Street is furnished with the same blue carpets, black desks, and reproductions of early Japanese woodcuts as the other offices around the globe. Tokyo being eight hours ahead of London, the telex to start buying Blenders' shares discreetly was on the desk of the chief manager, Mr Yaichiro Kaburagi, when he arrived on Thursday morning. More accustomed to buying Japanese shares for London institutions moving funds out of the weak British economy into the stronger Japanese one, he was a little uncertain how best to proceed. Cautiously, he telephoned the investment manager of a merchant bank where he lunched frequently: "Is there," he enquired, "any London broker with a special knowledge of Blenders' business?"

"Braithwaites are the company's brokers, old chap. They are very close to them."

Mr Kaburagi sensed a danger in this closeness. "There has been much selling. Was that from Braithwaites?"

"Lord, no. They've probably done a little but they are basically trying to keep the price up. Miller & Bromley – everyone calls them M and B – are the biggest sellers. They seem to think Blenders is going bust."

"That is most interesting. Thank you. Thank you very much."

"We've had a turn-up for the books this morning," Miller & Bromley's dealing partner announced at lunch. "The Japs have given us an order to buy Blenders. That means a buying commission on top of the selling commission on that stock we've been pushing out. And with the little yellow men there helping to support the price, we'll shake out a lot more than we ever could on a falling market."

"Let's get out of the City," said Frank when he called Sarah that same morning. "Can you meet me in the Gay Hussar in Greek Street? I know it's out of the City but it's only four stops from Bank on the Central Line." Sarah, who was coming to like the thought of Frank very much, would happily have gone fourteen stops for lunch with him.

The contrast offered in the Gay Hussar between Imperial Austro-Hungarian trappings on the walls and left-wing publishers and politicians at the tables always intrigued her, while the richly-cooked Hungarian food seasoned with dill and sweet paprika reminded her of some of Marina's specialities seen from a different culinary angle. "I can never understand why it hasn't got a star in Michelin," she said to Frank.

"Thank goodness it hasn't – we'd never get a table. Now, tell me the worst about our image: are we condemned asset-strippers or do people see any good in us at all?"

"I did a quick audit this morning – over half the people I spoke to in the City thought you could improve your image by making more of what you do for workers and customers rather than stressing what you achieve for shareholders."

"But damn it, the City are the shareholders."

"Yes, but they believe it's good politics to make a show of always putting the other interests first."

"Well, if it's presentation we're talking about, that's not too difficult – provided we don't tell Tim he's got to clear his marketing plan with the Consumers' Association or have shop stewards on the Board."

By the time the cheese pancakes and the strong black coffee arrived, Sarah knew that she wanted to see more of Frank.

CHAPTER VII

Braithwaites' chief dealer, who combines the cunning of an East End barrow boy with the mien of a retired major general, called James on the following Monday from the floor of the Stock Exchange: "Looks to me as though there's something going on in Blenders, sir. There's been a lot of selling but the price keeps trying to get better. I'm just back from lunch with 'Weasel' (a respected member of the Stock Exchange Council). According to him one broker has been putting huge lines of Blenders' shares through the market: he wouldn't say who, but it must be M & B. Everyone knows they're sellers. Not only have they found a buyer, it looks as though there could be another buyer around as well – a careful one. He's using several brokers to cover his tracks."

"I was afraid of this," said James, "keep me in touch. What's the price now?"

"180p in the middle – well up from last week's 140p. At this rate it looks as though we should soon be able to do some of last week's orders to sell at 200p."

"Don't deal without referring to me. I'll check with the clients and see if they still want to sell. If there could be more in this than just a 'dead-cat' bounce, they may decide to sit tight."

James asked Milo to come to the partners' room. "You'd better get on to Andrew and warn him that it looks as though someone is building up a stake in Blenders. Possibly even two people. Ask him if they've heard anything or had any feelers and say I'm having a word with Hamchilds, their merchant bank."

The intelligence from Braithwaites deepened the collective gloom at Blenders. It was George Nunnelly who decided firmly that there should be a Board meeting on Wednesday morning to review the situation.

When the Earl of Glencorres, with a touch of acerbity, said from his Chester Square flat that he had not expected to go to Edinburgh again so soon, Nunnelly tactfully suggested Braithwaites' offices, which would allow James Murray to be present.

Somewhat mollified at the concession on the place, the Earl was nevertheless still ruffled by the short notice. He reflected that if he belonged to a trade union he would certainly be claiming overtime and wondered if he should not re-negotiate his contract to cover payment for extra days.

The Wednesday meeting was better attended than the emergency one the previous week – two of the four missing barons had returned hurriedly from South Africa. The other two had sent, from hotels in Hawaii and Thailand, where they were with their wives, messages of confidence in their colleagues, saying they were available if urgently required.

The Earl opened the meeting with a brief summary of events:

"George has been trying to quantify what the cost of the unfortunate 'Mountain Mist' contract could be next year. While everything must depend on the dollar exchange rate, it looks pretty certain that there will be another substantial loss. However, the National Scottish Bank has confirmed that it will provide banking facilities on the security of our bonded stocks until then.

"It seems, however, that we may be under pressure from

a different quarter. James Murray is the best person to tell us about this."

James quite enjoyed talking to directors en bloc; unlike some of his clients, they made good listeners and they seldom argued back. "Thank you, Chairman. Gentlemen, as you probably know, we here have been trying to rally the troops and prevent the share price collapsing. Naturally, if somebody gives us an order to sell, we must execute it. But the advice we have been giving our clients is that they should stick with the shares. Other houses have taken a different line – that is, after all, what makes a market. As a result, there has been very heavy activity in Blenders' shares. I don't know how many changed hands since you announced there would be a loss, but my guess is between 15 and 20 per cent.

"Normally selling on that scale after a pessimistic statement should drive the price right down – our research department thought it might not rally until it got towards 100p. As it is, it turned at 140p and was 190p when I checked just now. The institutions will not buy heavily in the uncertain hope of profit recovery in two or three years' time, particularly not when the price is rising, so the most likely assumption must be that one – or possibly more – buyers are building up a stake in Blenders with a view either to obtaining control or at least a holding big enough to influence the group's policies."

"You mean," queried Andrew, "that there could be a takeover bid?"

"It looks the most likely explanation."

"Good Lord! How dreadful. But there's never been any suggestion of this before."

"In the past Blenders was a large and reasonably successful company in a specialised industry and the strong share price was the company's best defence. Blenders is now, in the short-term at least, a patently unsuccessful company – but with just that potential for recovery which attracts a predator."

"Thank you, James," said Glencorres. "Well, gentlemen, as we seem to be under attack, we had better review our defences. George, how many shares does the Board control and then James, perhaps, could give us an idea of how many are in friendly hands."

"Starting with the directors," said George, tactfully omitting that Glencorres himself had no more than the minimum 1,000, "much the biggest shareholder is Andrew with 10 per cent, then Luke has about 3½ per cent and the remainder of the Board a little over 5 per cent."

"As far as we can tell from the register, various institutions – some we know well, others scarcely at all – have about 45 per cent and private shareholders the remaining 35 per cent plus."

"James, how would the institutions react to a bid?"

"You must remember that the whole business of managing money has got so competitive that the old notion of shareholder loyalty scarcely exists among institutions now. I sometimes think their horizons have shrunk to their ranking in next month's league table of capital growth. And after all the selling there has been, the register will be out of date: it'll be weeks before the transfers come in and we know who is still with us and who's baled out. I imagine most of the selling has been the institutions: private shareholders are usually more loyal, I would think particularly so in the case of Blenders as many are in Scotland and will be motivated by nationalism as well. But to make sure of them, we'll probably have to take on a PR agency like that place where my goddaughter Sarah works, Leo Hudson's – although I fear he'll probably want to put you on the box, Chairman."

This was not at all to the Earl's liking – although it could, he calculated, almost certainly justify a higher fee – so he returned briskly to the arithmetic: "If the Board can muster nearly 20 per cent, and the bulk of the private shareholders and at least the Scottish institutions stay with us, then we should be in quite a strong position."

It was at this stage that Andrew felt bound to disclose the option he had given Forde Jamieson on his shares.

"Good God!" exploded Dougal. "You have the nerve to criticise me for taking risks trying to get brand leadership in the American market, then you endanger our control of the company by getting involved in a hare-brained resort development, which is a notorious road to bankruptcy."

"That's not a very helpful comment, Dougal," put in Luke, "particularly as it was your misjudgement which started the trouble. James, what do you make of the Forde Jamieson option?"

"It sounds odd to me. Tim Weston didn't get where he is by being altruistic. It only makes sense if he's going to bid himself or is warehousing – that's City jargon for building up a block of shares with the intention of selling them on, at a profit, to a bidder. But now I think of it he is a likely candidate. His next move has to be a big one: Andrew, would the option lapse if you were to repay the loan?"

"I believe so: the loan is on an overdraft basis and the option is valid for my lifetime only. I made that a condition."

James took the initiative: "As a matter of urgency, Chairman, may I ask whether one of Blenders' banks would be prepared to take over the loan? There is a problem that the sums are large and a number of banks have singed their fingers on resort lending recently. But there is the security of the Blenders' shares as well: they are entirely yours, are they, Andrew? I'm surprised they weren't in trust because of death duties."

"My father gave them to me in good time well before he died. He couldn't stand trusts – said you landed up in the hands of a whole lot of old-maid solicitors."

"Might have been no bad thing," snorted Dougal.

James interposed guilelessly, "Yes, but handing them over is not so easy now with Capital Transfer Tax. If you died suddenly wouldn't three-quarters of your holding have to be sold to meet the tax?"

"True, but I think I'm in fairly good health and I'll take out an insurance policy to cover the tax just as soon as the Bormona business is straight. And if a bank may be going to take over the loan, then I think it all the more important that I go to Bormona tomorrow as planned to check progress for myself. Also Tim Weston's partner, Frank Higgins, is coming with us and it will give me a chance to talk the situation over with him." Andrew suddenly felt desperately tired of boardroom wranglings and ached for the solitude and simplicity of white mountains and blue skies.

"George," said the Earl, turning to his finance director, "have you any other suggestions for repelling boarders?"

"The usual way is an optimistic profit forecast into which you hurl every possible stock profit and all the little things you've been keeping back over the years just in case. After our statement last week we are scarcely in a position to do this convincingly." Glum nods acknowledged this point.

"However, if we are prepared to take drastic measures – and let's face it, the company is haemorrhaging – I see one possibility. Although Blenders owns the shares of 'Mountain Mist', making it a wholly owned subsidiary, it is still technically a separate company. We could pay off its borrowings and wind the company up, pleading that the contract made it insolvent and that the bankruptcy laws have left us no option. Then Mabalian would have to deal with the liquidators and could whistle for his whisky."

The dead silence which greeted this was broken by an explosive "You must be mad," from Dougal. "Not in the least," said George coolly, "just taking advantage of the protection afforded by limited liability."

Andrew joined the objectors, "This is what you expect of some back-street operator, not a major group like us. We might not have, strictly speaking, a legal liability to our subsidiaries, but surely we have a moral one."

"Can we afford moral liabilities in our predicament?" countered George. "I'm not saying we ought to do it, that's for the whole Board to decide; I'm saying that it's something we could do."

"There's something else we could do," Dougal had by now mastered his fury sufficiently to speak coherently: "Consider a suggestion Joseph Mabalian put to me last week which would solve everything. The details haven't been worked out yet and I wasn't going to mention it until they were. But now obviously I must. Briefly, he is prepared to sell Likkermart to Blenders in exchange for Blenders' shares. Then the distributor's profits on the 'Mountain Mist' deal would come into the group and everything would be all right again. And as Joseph owns two-thirds of the Likkermart shares, there would be no problem on his side of the deal. He's in London at the moment and wants to meet the Board. I'm lunching with him today."

"A deal on that scale would need the agreement of Blenders' shareholders," James put in quickly, "and securing that might not be the usual formality in these circumstances. You should also realise that on present values it would make Mr Mabalian the biggest shareholder in Blenders; roughly it would give him something like 15 per cent of the company."

"He comes into this boardroom over my dead body," interjected Andrew with uncharacteristic vehemence. "I can't stand that oily crook – apart from which my friends in America say that he's in some pretty unsavoury rackets."

A sacrilegious knock at the door shattered the tension. Milo entered quietly and passed a note to James: the others looked towards him expectantly. "Gentlemen, the Sonkay Spirits Company of Japan has just bought 5 per cent of Blenders' shares in the market. The Board of Sonkay say they have the fullest confidence in the Blenders Board and look forward to friendly discussions."

"About their bloody malt contract, I don't doubt," hissed Dougal, "cunning yellow bastards. We should never have supplied them in the first place."

Milo returned to the room. "There is a Mr Seizo on the

telephone. He says he is Chairman of Sonkay Spirits and that he would like to speak to Lord Glencorres."

"Could you put him through, please," said Glencorres.

"Good morning, Mr Seizo. We have just seen your announcement and my colleagues and I have been discussing it. Naturally, we should be happy to meet you. You are in Germany now and will be in London this evening. Unfortunately I shall not be available until Monday. Would that suit you? Fine. My secretary will contact you at your hotel on Friday and arrange the details. Thank you, Mr Seizo. Good-bye."

"Well, gentlemen," turning back to his colleagues, "it seems we live in interesting times. I suggested Monday to give us time to resolve, if possible, the option over Andrew's shares." Turning to the director of the National Scottish Bank, "Hamish, perhaps you could be so kind as to discuss this with Andrew after the meeting, which is, I believe, now concluded."

On the Stock Exchange the announcement brought pandemonium. The market scented an epic struggle: those who had sold clamoured to buy back and those who never owned the shares suddenly discovered Blenders' unique attractions to a foreign buyer. Within minutes the price shot to 240p and the salesmen at Miller & Bromley, who the day before had been cataloguing Blenders' woes at 180p, now rated the shares, with a bidder in the offing, as well worth buying at 240p.

The headline writers enjoyed themselves that night: "Yellow Peril in the Stills" screamed the *Daily News* on Thursday. The *Times* had a second leader on the importance of retaining the ownership of key exporting industries and Scottish Members of Parliament tabled questions asking whether it could be a condition of giving permission to foreign companies to buy into Scottish industry that they should not increase unemployment.

CHAPTER VIII

"What do we do now?" Tim Weston sounded out Frank as they looked at the Thursday morning financial columns. Frank spoke thoughtfully, "I'm not sure we need to rush anything. The Japanese are cautious and take a long time to reach a decision. They're still highly sensitive to 'Yellow Peril' headlines and I'm not at all convinced they want to bid for the whole company. It's more likely that they are worried about their malt contract and see a 5 per cent holding as a good bargaining counter. If we guaranteed their malt contract, they might well come in with us."

"You could be right," Tim sounded relieved. "We'd better try to have a meeting to sound them out: we can probably arrange it through Monawa, who do most of their business. Meanwhile, Frank, how do we stand at the moment?"

"We have picked up nearly 15 per cent in the market. Assuming we exercise our option on Andrew's stock (a deal about which Frank had growing qualms) that would give us 25 per cent. Institutions who have always sided with us in the past have 6 per cent: if we can get the Japs on our side, we'll be in a strong position."

"We might find we get support from other Board members, perhaps to the tune of another 3½ per cent," Tim added noncommittally.

"You mean Luke Grey's holding? Why on earth should he side with us?"

"Andrew isn't the only vulnerable member of that

Board, but let's wait and see. It's more important to talk to the Japs first."

"If we do get Blenders, what about the Likkermart contract?"

"That's the least of the problems. We tell Mabalian, who's a rough customer and understands straight talk, that either he re-negotiates the contract or we will put 'Mountain Mist' into liquidation. He'll talk. Now I think I'll have a word with Kaburagi at Monawa's. Meanwhile, I don't think we should pay over 240p in the market. I don't want to alarm Andrew any further by getting in to the trigger area for his option just yet."

"Mr Kaburagi, good morning, this is Timothy Weston, Chairman of Forde Jamieson. I believe Sonkay is a client of yours. If I may speak confidentially, as it is not generally known, our clients also have substantial holdings in Blenders. If there were an opportunity I think it would be advantageous if we could meet privately with the principals of Sonkay." He paused. "Mr Seizo is in London and coming to your office in half an hour. Excellent. Perhaps you would be so kind as to suggest a brief meeting here at noon: or we could come to your office if that would be more convenient. Thank you so very much."

At much the same time the chief general manager of the National Scottish Bank telephoned Blenders' finance director, George Nunnelly. "George, I'm afraid I can see problems on taking over that loan of Andrew's. We're very happy to support the company through its problems but we've had some bitter experience with resort developments: in fact the Board has ruled that we should not do any more. There are, of course, always exceptions for old clients, but there is the extra problem that Andrew's only collateral is his Blenders' shares. If the effect of the loan were to frustrate a bid for Blenders, then the share price could fall like a stone, leaving the Bank without proper cover for its loan. The only way around I can see is that Blenders guarantee the loan."

George drew his breath in sharply: "I don't like the sound of it. The company has no business, particularly in its present predicament, underwriting anything so high risk. I certainly couldn't do it off my own bat: I would want a Board ruling. Dougal's the only director here today, and I'll mention it to him. He's so desperate he would probably agree to anything, but I should be surprised if the others do. Andrew himself is very particular about things like this: he's always insisted that private ventures be kept separate from the company and he might well not agree. I don't see that we can give you an answer before next week. On the other hand, if we have a good meeting with the Japs on Monday, the fate of Andrew's shares may not be so important."

The Japanese contingent arrived punctually at Forde Jamieson's at noon. Mr Seizo, stocky, neatly grey-suited and bespectacled, his wide face and high cheekbones designed by Nature for impassivity, was accompanied by two colleagues of similar mien, who respectfully said nothing throughout the meeting. London living had made their escort, Mr Kaburagi, less conservative in dress and more outgoing in manner. After the ritual exchange of cards, Tim opened, "We are most honoured by your visit, Mr Seizo. As I mentioned to Mr Kaburagi in confidence, we, too, as a group, are large shareholders in Blenders. We are, if anything, slightly larger shareholders than you."

"I am surprised to learn it," countered Mr Seizo stiffly, "there has been no announcement, which I understand is required by your takeover rules."

"That is why I said 'as a group'. We control a number of different trusts here and no single one has as much as 5 per cent."

"I did not know," Mr Seizo's lips had become perceptibly thinner, "that your rules allowed so much flexibility."

Tim made light of the point. "It's more a matter of understanding the system. We are very concerned about developments at Blenders," he continued smoothly, "Perhaps if we were to come to an understanding together, we might be able to bring about some necessary changes on the Board to our mutual advantage. As it is, I believe you have some trading contracts to renew with them."

Mr Seizo spoke carefully. "Naturally, we must consider every proposal. But we have great confidence in our friends on the Board of Blenders. Our shareholding shows our support for them: in Japan we are familiar with the problems which can arise in capturing a foreign market – they are never serious in the end. I hope when we meet with the Blenders' Board on Monday we can offer them your support also. That would show that you, too, are intelligent and far-sighted businessmen. And now, Mr Weston, if you will excuse us, we are due at the Japanese Embassy for lunch in thirty minutes and must go through your famous London traffic, a joy we in Tokyo share with you."

Smiling mechanically, and with many expressions of esteem, the group withdrew.

"That's the brush-off, Japanese style," was Frank's verdict. "They don't have people who operate like us and what little they know of us they don't like. In Japan the takeover battle is unknown: the stock market exists solely to provide funds for industry. If the control of a company is going to change hands that's organised cosily by Japan Inc."

"I think this means," said Tim decisively, "that we must advance our timing. Today is Thursday: the sooner we have Andrew's stock firmly in our hands, the happier I shall be. We mustn't give the opposition a chance to get him off the hook. Meanwhile, we must carry on as normal. Frank, I think you should go to Bormona as planned this afternoon: it would look suspicious if you pulled out suddenly."

Frank nodded, but his pleasure at the prospect of three

days with Sarah was clouded by his discomfort at the bank's tactics with her father. He had come to like Andrew and respect his straightforwardness: now he dreaded Sarah's anger and contempt when she realised the double game he had been playing.

At its regular Thursday investment meeting the Providential Assurance decided to sell its substantial holding in Blenders' shares if it could get 255p for them. Forde Jamieson, which had refused to pay more than 240p previously, bought them.

CHAPTER IX

On Thursday mid-morning in the departure lounge for Nice a troubled Andrew came straight to the point. "Frank, we must talk about this share option. I must say I thought it was a bit of a formality on Tim's part, something to satisfy the auditors. This business of the Japs makes it very tricky for all of us and puts me in a hell of a spot with my Board."

"And if you're really concerned about your image," added Sarah, "this will improve your reputation for sharp dealing but not much else."

"Certainly the Japs have taken us completely by surprise." Frank stuck carefully to the literal truth.

"Perhaps," Sarah's tone became notably drier, "but the market is also saying that Forde Jamieson is warehousing Blenders' shares and some of the brokers think you might be going to make a bid yourselves."

Frank paused. "Tim Weston keeps his important cards very close to his chest, even with his own Board. I think, Andrew, the best thing would be to come in and talk with him as soon as we get back."

"Splendid," said a relieved Andrew, "that's just what I would like to do. Let's say no more about the whole affair until then and instead make the most of the mountains."

The Baies des Anges apartments, an incongruous cross-section of the pyramids perched by the Cote d'Azur, signalled to the regulars in the descending plane the proximity of Nice. "I always start to get excited at this stage." Sarah leaned across Frank to peer through the window: the brush of her body against his sent tremors to the depths of his stomach. "I know that in three hours we'll be up in the mountains."

In the mild winter warmth on the tarmac at Nice, their heavy boots, bulky anoraks and awkward skis were oddly out of place but once they reached the foothills in the white VW bus, emblazoned with BORMONA 2000, the jollity of the mountains began to infect the group. On the journey Andrew listened eagerly to Michel, chief instructor of the nascent skiing school and the man on the spot he trusted most. The contractors were making good progress with the next stage: they had sent an excellent manager and, provided he stayed, it looked as though everything should be ready for the next season. The guests who were in the hotel already open were full of praise and promising to return. It had snowed at the beginning of the week and now conditions were perfect. The piste was packed but never icy, just enough melted at midday to produce a spray on a good turn. The powder snow was a dream, Michel said: a deep crisp fluff but with a firm base below covering most of the rocks and boulders.

Two hours turning and twisting up narrow roads hacked into the hillside brought them to the edge of the snow line at St Croix du Monte, the village which had been the highest local habitation before the building of Bormona. They stopped for a grog in the warm, steamy café where Andrew was at once monopolised by the proprietor who was hoping for a concession in the development. As he looked around, Frank wondered whether the mountains were as healthy a place as city dwellers imagined. Apart from the prevalence of goitre, squints and wall-eyes, two of the drinkers betrayed symptoms of mild idiocy. It might, he supposed, on the other hand just be the results of inbreeding in the enclosed valley.

They transferred to a jeep with snow chains on the tyres and set off up the pass: it was dusk when they reached the broad-bottomed snow bowl of the resort. On one side the buildings were a honeycomb of brightness: opposite, long fingers of light made by the lifts probed up into the hillside. "It doesn't look so good by day," said Andrew, "you can see then that it's only half finished. One hotel tower and the first of the self-catering apartment blocks are complete and there's a food supermarket. When it's all done there'll be three hotel towers, another bigger apartment block, a shopping complex, church, ice rink, swimming pool and sauna. We're staying in the hotel as they're still decorating our apartment."

The hotel's comfort belied its unpromising appearance in which raw concrete, plastic, and primary colours predominated. The beds were soft, the heating was adjustable and everything in the compact bathroom functioned. More importantly, the cooking in the dining room was superb. Was it a first sign of age, Frank wondered, that if it came to a choice between, on the one hand, the extended magnificence of the Lech-Zurs St Anton ski-circuit combined with heavy Austrian dumplings and thin red wine, and, on the other hand, this more modest French terrain, but accompanied by rare steaks, perfect salads and good claret, he would find it increasingly difficult to decide? Sarah broke into his thoughts saying, "The disco has been opened since I was last here – would you like to see what it's like?" His delight in this proposal brought home to Frank with a jolt that Sarah's company far outranked any other present pleasure. The probability that an attraction, which he was beginning to sense might be mutual, would be extinguished when the trap Tim Weston had set for Andrew was sprung, quickened his response: "I'd love to."

"In that case I'm off to bed," said Andrew. "Michel says there's perfect powder on the North face of Mont Triste. There's no lift yet and it's quite a haul up there. The hire shop is open till ten tonight so I must go and get skins for my old climbing skis now. Then I'll need an early night; it's a long haul up."

"Shall we come too?" asked Sarah.

"Thank you, my dear, but I have a lot on my mind at the moment and I find that going off on my own gives me a chance to think it all through. Enjoy yourselves."

The disco was intimate, the music below headache volume and the lighting only mildly disorienting. Sarah danced in an easy, relaxed manner and with a responsiveness which gave Frank confidence. As it was Sarah's first visit, a bottle of Taittinger Rosé arrived with the compliments of the management. "I do like pink champagne," said Sarah dreamily, "it anaesthetises all my inhibitions. The old rogue only sent it as a way of keeping Daddy sweet, but now that it's here let's enjoy it."

Afterwards they danced more closely and later, when they got out of the lift, Sarah took a light but firm hold on Frank's hand and led him into her room. Their first kiss was long, exploratory and deeply satisfying. Sarah, still just in control, unbuttoned Frank's shirt, stroked his erect brown nipples, then began to tease them playfully with her tongue. Frank reacted passionately, his kisses becoming increasingly urgent as his mouth roamed over her body. Sighing with pleasure, Sarah clung to him as they sank back on the bed.

They woke late, sated and warmly affectionate; by the time they came down to breakfast Andrew had already set forth, leaving a message that he would be back in the early afternoon. Michel was meeting him at the bottom of the run where it hit the main road and they would probably have lunch in St Croix du Mont.

Sarah said, "I almost wish we'd insisted on going. If you like deep snow there's nothing to beat it. Only the enthusiasts know about Mont Triste but once the lift reaches up there it'll be flattened and become another piste. Now you have to climb on skins for an hour. The first descent is tremendous – a long, wide slope, but quite steep. In powder you can make a track there any travel poster would love to use. Then there's a narrow run through the trees, some long traverses and finally a series of gentle meadows where you can do every turn in the book. But you have to be careful: there are treacherous gulleys which are difficult to see. You finish on the main road about an hour's drive away – that's where Michel is going to meet Daddy today. If we feel strong enough," a slightly self-conscious smile, "we might try it ourselves tomorrow. Now let's concentrate on piste-bashing and getting our ski-legs back."

At the top of the lift Frank caught his breath in a spasm of pleasure at the diamantine brilliance of the fresh snow glittering in the bright morning sun. Although the sky was flawless azure Frank noticed in the distance the faint blue haze on the pines which signals a change in the weather; but the morning's enjoyment, at least, was secure. Sarah proved a good skier, turning neatly and adroitly, always under control. Frank attacked the slope more aggressively, taking greater risks; to his surprise, when they raced, their times were nearly equal.

Happy and exhausted they were sitting before lunch in the sun at the crowded ice bar, suffused by that sense of well-being induced by vigorous exercise followed by a cool drink. They were beginning their second when the hotel manager, incongruously dark-suited and pale-featured, picked his way through the booted crowd to them carrying an envelope. "Miss MacLintock, do you know where your father is? There's a telex from London marked 'Urgent'." Frank's stomach was assaulted by a sudden spasm of fear and guilt.

"He should be back later in the afternoon: leave it with me, please."

Sarah turned to Frank, "I suppose they're like telegrams: they should be opened at once in case we can do anything."

She ripped open the envelope and read.

"Christ! Frank, what the hell is this about?"

Forde Jamieson have just bid 280p a share for Blenders. They claim their trusts already own 17 per cent of the shares and to have an option over a further 10 per cent.

Milo

"That's our 10 per cent isn't it?" Sick inside, Frank could only nod. "You shit. You fucking, two-faced, double-dealing shits. You set Daddy up, didn't you? 'The option's a formality – just to keep the accountants happy.' How you must have been laughing at him. You didn't want me – you wanted my father's shares and you'll use any means to get them." Her face distorted with fury, her hand shot out and slapped Frank's face hard, then, before he could recover, she stumbled blindly through the thicket of boots and skis back to the hotel.

Frank's first reaction was a large whisky. His next was to go to his room and telephone Tim Weston in London. "What the bloody hell is going on? Why come out with the bid now?"

"I can see it's a bit tricky for you," Tim after all knew nothing about Sarah, "but we had to rush it out, because the Japs came into the market again this morning and pushed the price up to 260p. As they seem more likely to side with the Board, we had to announce our bid before they picked up any more. Luckily, we managed to get another 1 per cent in the market below 280p before we made the announcement. Under the rules we can't buy stock over our bid price and, of course, the market's gone mad. The jobbers are short and have marked the price up to 300p. For the moment the Japs have gone to ground: it'll take them a while to decide their next move so things may quieten down this afternoon. I think the line to take with Andrew is that it's the Japs or us, and which would he rather have? Anyhow, with our option on his stock he hasn't got much choice, so he may as well lie back and enjoy it."

Chapter X

Frank's solitary lunch in the hotel restaurant was interrupted by a worried Michel. "Where is Mlle Sarah? Two hours I have been waiting for Mr MacLintock. Always he is punctual. We must climb and look."

Frank called Sarah's room, "Your father seems to be missing. Michel and I are going to look for him."

"Oh God. I'll come too. I'll meet you in the hire shop to pick up climbing skis."

As they started up the mountain the Day-glo blue of the Alpine sky was now flecked by the trailing wisps of cloud which, together with the moist breath of the Mistral, heralded a change in the weather. The atmospheric heaviness increased Frank's sense of foreboding, extinguishing the pleasure he would normally have taken in the isolation of the off-piste slopes. The climb was a silent affair: breath is precious at 10,000 feet.

As they reached the shoulder of Mont Triste the shadows were beginning to lengthen but Andrew's solitary tracks were clearly visible. Michel led the descent, then swung to a sudden stop as he rounded the slope to the main North face. "*Incroyable, une avalanche.* Never has there been one on this slope." The ominous fan spewed down the mountainside, breaking the smooth surface with its sickening cargo of snow, rocks and rubble. Michel schussed to the point where Andrew's tracks entered the avalanche, half way down the long slope. "*Vite.* We must search. We have no poles. We must use our sticks."

Unfastening the baskets off the bottom, they systematically dug their sticks into the snow. It was Sarah who cried: "God! I've touched something. I think I've found him."

Tearing at the snow with their gloved hands, it took them ten minutes to reach the dead, entombed Andrew. Frank held Sarah very tight. "I don't understand it, I don't understand it," she sobbed hysterically. "Daddy was always so careful. He had a horror of avalanches, and never took risks. And, Michel, you never get avalanches on this slope, do you?"

"Never before."

Frank peered up the shadowed mountainside. "It's difficult to see, but there's something not right about this. Avalanches usually start on the surface, then pick up the snow as they accelerate downhill. From here, it looks as though it was started by a huge chunk straight out of the middle of that overhang at the top. It's definitely odd. I'm going to look. You and Michel go on down."

"There is not time." Michel knew how fast darkness falls in the mountains. "To reach the top is an hour. Then it will be hard to see and the track in the woods is dangerous."

"I know you're right Michel, but I must go and look. It's terribly suspicious and if we wait until tomorrow the snow will hide everything. Sarah, you and Michel ski on, I'll follow."

Sarah was adamant: "I'm not leaving you to go down on your own in the dark. But for God's sake be quick."

"*Bien*, I wait too," said Michel.

A crater three metres wide which had blown away a whole section of the overhang rewarded Frank for an hour's leg-straining climb. Although it was by now dusk, the scorch marks in the snow were still visible. "Who on earth?" thought Frank, "and how?" For no ski tracks led to the crater: the only sets on the mountainside were Andrew's, his, Sarah's and Michel's.

Once a quick search had yielded nothing in the way of shrapnel or mechanism, Frank started off downhill. It had begun to snow and the cold which had already stiffened the hairs in his nostrils caught sharply at his throat so that even breathing became painful. By now it was so dark that it was almost impossible to see the contours of the slope and picking the right spot to turn became increasingly guess-work. His first tumble, when the ground fell away unexpectedly on a turn, was into the slope and mild: the next when he failed to spot a mound threw him hard downhill in a flurry of loose skis and sticks. Back upright, he negotiated gingerly until he reached Sarah and Michel. "There was a crater. Some sort of explosion. Tell you more at the bottom – if we ever reach it."

Michel led the trio. The snow was falling more thickly and the darkness now almost total. "We must tie something white round the arm: it will help to see. And we must stay close: soon we reach the woods."

By daylight the woods were a challenging run. The narrow path left little room for manoeuvre and the speed on the steep sections called for keen nerves and a quick eye for the next bend.

"We must snowplough," said Michel, and the group inched its way down in a position which makes out-of-condition muscles swiftly quiver with pain.

An agonising hour later they emerged. "The worst is over," said Michel, "still we take great care." But shock, fatigue and the strain on her muscles progressively weakened Sarah's control over her skis. She collapsed slowly in front of Frank. "I can't go on. I'm finished." Frank in reply slapped her face to sharpen her senses. "Don't be crazy. It's not much further."

"Why should I go on? I loved my father more than anyone. And now he's dead. I want to die too."

"And I want you to live, you fool!" yelled Frank.

The wind had got up and the snow was now driving into their eyes.

Sarah and Frank stayed as close as safety permitted to Michel, who was skiing by the memories and instincts of a lifetime. As they were traversing a steep slope a sudden shriek echoed from Sarah as her ski caught an edge on a rock outcrop and she slid, headlong and helpless, down the slope.

"Do we ski down that way?" Frank asked.

"No, we go over the next shoulder."

"Then wait." Guided by Sarah's cries, Frank sidestepped down to find her wet and shaken, half buried in a snowdrift.

"I can't get up: my skis are right in the bank."

"Well, they say you should stay in the fall-line: have you broken anything?"

"I don't think so."

"Then lie still and I'll dig you out."

Exhaustion, cold and the shocks of the day again attacked Sarah. "I'll never make it back up to Michel. I'm done for. Please save yourself Frank, please."

"If I have to carry you, I'll get you up there. We'll sidestep up." Holding out his lower stick: "You hang on to this: it'll make it easier."

Painfully they fought their way back up, guided by the path of Sarah's fall and Michel's shouts from above. As they reached him Sarah gasped, "I doubt if I shall ever see a warm bed again."

"*Courage*," said Michel, "there is not long to go. Stay close."

Twenty minutes later they reached the road where Michel's assistant, incoherent with worry, was waiting with a Land Rover. "Thank God!" said Frank. "Thank God! I never want an experience like that again."

Sarah slept fitfully on Frank's shoulder on the way back. When they reached the hotel, Michel said, "I will tell the Gendarmerie. Tomorrow we make statements and go for the body."

As Michel left, Sarah demanded of Frank, "Tell me again what you found up there."

"I think the avalanche was deliberately started but I'll tell you everything when you have had a hot bath and recovered," was his firm reply. "Then I'll have our dinner sent up to your room: I'll be there within the hour."

The hot water relaxed Sarah's tensed muscles but her mind was battered by emotions warring for dominance – shock, despairing grief at the image of her father's corpse entombed in snow, hatred of Frank's duplicity tempered by grateful love for his courage on the mountainside. She called a truce for rational assessment. Despair would be softened by time but what did she now feel for Frank? The duplicity, she guessed, was not his plan and must in any event have begun before they first met. "Poor Frank, how he must have hated himself." At least his heroism that afternoon had been personal and selfless. Or had it been? Would evidence of murder strengthen Forde Jamieson's position? Had it been a striving banker or a shamed lover who scaled the slope? Sarah, clear-minded as she was, could not bring herself to believe that Frank would have risked his and indeed *her* life to get a move ahead in the bid game. Stifling doubts, she decided that it had been for her sake.

The grief and torment had left Sarah's face pale and drawn when, changed into a skirt and jumper, she opened the door to Frank an hour later.

"I tried to call my mother but there was no reply, so I sent a cable. Frank, what happened up there today? You think it was deliberate?"

"Without doubt. There is an overhang at the top where a huge weight of snow had built up. Somebody had planted explosive there which must have dislodged literally tons of snow down the steepest part of the slope. Poor Andrew didn't stand a chance."

"But who? And why?" Hysteria was creeping into Sarah's voice, "Daddy never hurt a soul. And he didn't have an enemy."

"Let's start with the how. It was clear from what I saw up there that this was a professional job, not a local who might have had a grudge about the development."

The arrival of a waiter with dinner interrupted him. "I

don't know about you but I need something to drink – what about a whisky?"

As they sat down at the small table, Frank continued, "From the moment I saw the crater I have been trying to puzzle things out. In the first place, whoever planted the explosive must have known that Andrew was going to be up there today: the mountains cannot be riddled with booby traps in the hope that Andrew might ski by. But Andrew only decided yesterday afternoon to go, and only a handful of people knew about it. For a start, that narrows the list of suspects. I suppose whoever is responsible banked on no one climbing up to the top this evening – it was certainly foolhardy. By tomorrow morning the snowfall would have covered the evidence.

"The other thing that baffles me is that although it must have been planted there since last night at the earliest, there were no other tracks in the snow. How did it get there? And how was it triggered just as Andrew went by? I can think of only one explanation which fits: whoever did it came by helicopter."

"But there isn't one in Bormona," objected Sarah.

"True. But Italy's only just the other side of the peaks. And as I remember there are several helicopters in Cervula, which isn't much more than ten minutes' flight away. They could have set off the charge by remote control when Andrew was skiing down – or possibly they might have relied on a trip wire. We won't find the answer to that until the snow melts but maybe we can find out now who hired the helicopter."

Swiftly Sarah asked the telephone operator to get Inspector Jummel of the gendarmerie in St Croix du Mont. "He and Daddy had become great friends – and I know he'll do everything to help."

"Inspector Jummel. You've heard? Thank you very much. It's absolutely dreadful – but I am not sure that it was an accident." Swiftly Sarah explained Frank's theory. "Inspector, I know there will have to be an official investigation but that takes time. If you could straightaway ask your colleagues in Cervula who hired a helicopter today, that might give us a very important clue before the trail goes cold . . . Thank you, thank you. Until morning then."

"He's going to check up on his local network and he will come to see Michel and us tomorrow morning."

The prospect of action diverted Sarah's grief. As they ate dinner she challenged Frank: "Why did you climb back up this afternoon? Why did it matter enough to take the risk?

Frank paused before replying: "I haven't stopped to analyse it fully. To begin with, I love you. Then I hated myself for my part in Tim Weston's shabby plot to get your father's shares. And I had become fond of Andrew for himself, apart from the fact that he was your father. I knew there was something fishy and it made me blindly angry. I *had* to find out. But you must understand. It wasn't intellectual curiosity. You had been hurt and I had to know for your sake."

Relief flooded through Sarah but she contained it, just pressing Frank's hand, and continued: "Let's say you are right as to how it was done. That still leaves who and why."

"It was obviously the work of a professional, a paid hit-man," replied Frank. "Even if we get him we may never find out who hired him. So we must look for motive. You say Andrew had no personal enemies. It's unlikely that anyone in Bormona could have wanted to kill him: after all, he was keeping the whole place going. But Inspector Jummel will be the best person to tell us about that. That leaves Blenders. And I feel pretty sure that's where the key must be."

Sarah was appalled. She shouted harshly: "You mean he might have been killed because of those wretched shares? Take somebody's life for a few bits of paper?"

"They're more than bits of paper, they represent power and wealth. People have always been ready to kill for that."

The horrors of the day suddenly overwhelmed Sarah and, weeping hysterically, she flung herself into Frank's arms. "My poor father. My poor father. Oh, Frank, I did love him so. I'm so unhappy, so unhappy."

"Nothing we can do will bring him back. But I promise you as I love you, that I will do everything I can to find the killer. Now you must sleep. We are both exhausted and there will be a lot to do tomorrow."

That same Friday night in London, Luke lay in bed drawing on a contented, post-coital cigarette. He turned to look affectionately at Robin dozing beside him. He had seen perhaps too much of Robin since they met at Nelson's. Luke husbanded his emotions carefully, seldom allowing attachments to ripen into affairs. There was a danger of this happening with Robin for as well as being handsome and sexually athletic he possessed a mordant sense of humour which deeply appealed to Luke and which that evening had temporarily banished the worry of the Forde Jamieson bid.

Robin opened his eyes, leant over, and kissed Luke gently. "Love," he said, "I must confess something to you."

"You're not coming away for the weekend?"

"Try stopping me. No, it's something quite different. Do you remember when we met I told you I was twenty-one. Well, I'm not."

Luke laughed. "No one ever is. It's the golden age; for some people it lasts a long time. Though I must say you don't look twenty-three or four."

"I should bloody well hope not. I'm nineteen."

Luke sat straight upright in bed. His relaxed attitude towards his sex life owed much to his strict adherence to the letter of the law, which in Britain forbids sex between men if either is under 21.

"Why did you lie?"

"Well, I fancied you and I was afraid it might put you off."

Alert to the threat of blackmail, Luke probed cautiously: "Does being under age worry you?"

"Why should it, my love, but it does make me feel I can rely on you. Not for money, though: I'm no gold-digger. There's just one thing and I'm not quite sure how to ask. A friend of mine has a big business deal going and it would mean a lot to him if you could support him. Don't worry, it won't cost you. In fact it should be very profitable."

"No doubt you'll let me know," Luke spoke coolly.

"Of course I will, petal," replied Robin, his mouth moving towards Luke's groin as he eased across the bed.

CHAPTER XI

Although it was still snowing heavily on Saturday morning, Inspector Jummel arrived while Sarah and Frank were breakfasting. His olive complexion, cropped black head and neat moustache suggested the film-cliché French official; he was wearing a black tie, a mark of respect to the dead *patron*, with his weekend tweed jacket. Bowing to Sarah, he said, "Mademoiselle, my deepest condolences. We had a great affection for your father. He was a fine man and did much for the people here. If his death was not an accident, we shall discover the cause. Meanwhile, a party has left to bring the body down."

"What about the helicopters and Cervula?" put in Frank.

"Monsieur, we started enquiries last night: I have asked my colleague to call me here. But first, for I have a report to prepare for the examining magistrate, you must tell me what happened on the mountain yesterday. Coffee? That would be most kind. Thank you."

Swiftly Frank recounted the story of the crater. "It was good that you climbed to look, monsieur, for last night's snow will fill that crater. You found no metal, nothing?"

"It was getting dark and there was little time to search. But I could see that the snow was badly scorched."

The telephone gave the long imperious ring which characterises the French system. The Inspector answered it. "That is interesting. So, indeed. Fine. Can you call Franco in Cervula at once: the description may help them. And check where the car went in Nice."

Turning to Frank and Sarah, the Inspector asked, "Did you see Monsieur MacLintock talking to an Oriental here on Thursday evening? Did he say anything to you about meeting one?"

"Not a word," replied Sarah. "There are lots of them in the mountains these days but I cannot say that I noticed one in particular."

"A Korean, or someone using a Korean passport in the name of Nom Kay Pon, checked into the hotel on Thursday. People who saw him on the slopes say he is a phenomenal skier. He praised Bormona to the manager of the hotel, asking when Monsieur MacLintock would arrive as he wanted to discuss the development with him – he claimed to be involved in something similar in Japan. Then André in the hire shop saw him when Monsieur MacLintock went in to get climbing skis and skins on Thursday evening. The Korean started talking to Monsieur MacLintock, as happens in the mountains: André's English is not very good but he heard Mont Triste mentioned so probably your father talked about his route yesterday."

"Where is the Korean now?" asked Frank.

"That is what is so interesting. He checked out very late on Thursday and asked the manager to get a car to take him to Nice."

"Whereabouts in Nice?"

"My assistant is checking." The telephone pealed again. "The Avis office. *Bon.* Ask Etienne in Nice to send someone round there straightaway, get all the particulars and then phone me here. What did Cervula say? Franco is out but has left word that he hopes to have news soon. *Bon.*"

The Inspector turned to Sarah, "Mademoiselle, if we are on the right track, this shocking affair is the work of an outsider, not of a local. Who knew your father was coming here?"

"Lots of people," said Sarah. "It was not a secret. The people in his company – Blenders – knew and, of course, they knew in the Bormona London office."

"And in our bank," put in Frank.

"And at Braithwaites, too, I suppose," added Sarah. "Daddy said they had a board meeting there this week."

"So, it would have been easy for an enquirer to discover that your father was coming here. I can help you discover methods. But the motive lies outside this village. Who would gain from Monsieur MacLintock's death?"

Sarah looked tearfully blank. Frank put in tentatively, "Someone who didn't want Forde Jamieson to buy Blenders." Frank then sketched the bid and the terms of the option to the Inspector; "You see, the bank's option to buy Andrew's 10 per cent died with him. I've been thinking furiously about this and the only person with a motive is someone determined to stop us buying Blenders."

"Like the Japanese?" said Sarah.

"Like the Japanese," echoed Frank. "I don't believe they would go to these lengths."

"I'm not so sure," countered Sarah. "I remember Daddy saying to me on the way out that if the malt contract were not renewed, Sonkay would be in deep trouble for no one else in Scotland will supply them. Without Blenders malt they would have to abandon 'Imperial' which is their biggest selling brand."

"But why should they assume that if Forde's won we would freeze them out?"

"They couldn't be sure you wouldn't," countered Sarah. "But they knew that Blenders on its own was in their hands because of its cash problems. As part of Forde Jamieson it would be in a much stronger position. Come to think of it, why have Sonkay been buying Blenders' shares? They say it's to preserve Blenders' independence. But maybe they're planning a bid themselves. Don't you see, they couldn't afford to let our shares go to you. They're too crucial."

The telephone interrupted Sarah's train of speculation. The inspector reached for it. "Franco. *Bon giorno. Come stai*?" He listened attentively, interjecting questions in swift Italian. "*Bene. Mille grazia,* Franco." Turning to Frank, "I congratulate. Monsieur, it is as you thought. Yesterday morning an Oriental, this time with a Taiwanese passport, hired a helicopter in Cervula. He had a pilot's licence and said he wanted to take it out alone. He left his passport and a deposit of $50,000. People don't ask questions in Italy, particularly those parts within reach of the Swiss border, when that sort of money is involved. He returned the helicopter in the afternoon and hasn't been seen since. Almost certainly he will have driven to Milan, which is the nearest airport."

This conjecture was halted by another telephone peal. "Etienne? He returned the car to Milan airport last night. Now, can you call Giovanni Forco at the Carabinière in Milan – he knows me. Ask him if he can trace our Oriental, using either a Korean or a Taiwanese passport. If, as I think, he is a professional, he may have changed name and nationality again by now. But he cannot change his skin."

Turning to Frank and Sarah, he said, "We may be fortunate. The killer will think we are treating it as an accident, so he may not try too hard to cover his tracks. Even if he does, Giovanni will trace him. He is like a, as you say, truffle hound, that man. When I worked in Nice he was in Ravello: if I lost a suspect over the border, Giovanni would tell me in a day where he was. And I, too, have helped him. As soon as I hear from Giovanni, I shall contact you." And, bowing slightly, Inspector Jummel departed.

Fleet Street's alliterative sub-editors seized their opportunity that Saturday. "Blenders Beleaguered" offered the *Daily News*; "Battered Blenders Gets Bid" contributed the *Sentinel*. Under "Bid Battle For Blenders", Lux in the *Financial Times* self-indulgently exercised hindsight:

> "The opportunity offered by a unique collection of brand names, large stocks of maturing whisky, major management blunders and a depressed share price was bound to

be seized. The Japanese, to whom Blenders is a crucial supplier, appear to have been eyeing the opportunity but their characteristic caution puts them at a disadvantage in market manoeuvres. The interesting question is whether Forde Jamieson is a serious bidder or aiming to take a dealing profit on its stake: assimilating Blenders would certainly give its balance sheet a nasty hangover and would be taken as conclusive evidence that the company should be valued as an opportunistic conglomerate."

The *Daily Express* saw the issue in more clearcut and patriotic terms. "Tim Weston steps in to thwart the Japanese raiders. Yesterday the victor of many hard-fought takeover battles said, 'I am determined that this great British industry should not go the way of video, TV and radio manufacturing and end up dominated by the Orient'."

In the *Times* a second leader examined every argument meticulously and concluded by invoking the Monopolies Commission "for further consideration of the complex and far-reaching issues."

The politicians, scenting an issue larger than money, were vocal with ready-made opinions. To the Scottish Nationalist it was "a betrayal of our national heritage by London financiers": to the Labour Party it was "callous trafficking in jobs by City asset-strippers which should be discussed at once by the TUC": to the Tories it represented "the free play of market forces which should nevertheless be scrutinised for consideration of the National Interest" and to the Social Democrats it was an issue "on which we are urgently formulating a policy to take account of and reconcile the aspirations of workers, managers, customers and shareholders."

CHAPTER XII

"I think I should worry if one of them said something unpredictable." James peered over the top of his gold half-spectacles at Saturday breakfast with Clarissa in the light, picture-hung dining room of their country house in Oxfordshire. "It would be like the *Guardian* advocating capital punishment or the *Daily Telegraph* calling for a big expansion in social workers."

"If there weren't some certainties at our age in life, it would be really very trying," countered Clarissa, who in spite of this admission had preserved her slim, slight figure through three children. She then transferred her attention to murmuring endearments and feeding a piece of toast to Pang, who had perfected an appealing begging posture quite at variance with his vicious temperament. This domestic idyll was disturbed by the telephone. "If that's anyone asking us for drinks, say 'No'. I want some peace this weekend, now the children are safely immured in school."

James returned white-faced and said simply, "Andrew MacLintock has been killed in an avalanche in France."

"Oh God, no. Poor Marina. How dreadful. When?"

"Yesterday. That was Tim Weston on the phone."

"You mean that wheeler-dealer you always say Braithwaites distrust?"

"Yes, him. It seems he is staying at a house near here and one of his people who was in France with Andrew and Sarah has just telephoned."

"Does Marina know?"

"Yes. Sarah telephoned this morning and is coming back today. Weston says there is something he wants to talk to me about urgently so I asked him over for a drink before lunch today."

Clarissa, who held strong views on the sanctity of weekends, contented herself with, "So long as he is on his own and doesn't stay too long. Otherwise I'll set Pang on to him," giving the creature a wary pat on the head.

James's house, Elizabethan in origin, had been much altered and added to over the years, so that it had gradually settled into the landscape and now seemed as much part of the terrain as the trees which surrounded it and the formal yew hedges which backed Clarissa's herbaceous borders.

Tim drove fast up the drive in a large new Rolls Royce, taking in this evidence of old wealth and settled taste without resentment: his aims were still power rather than possessions. James led the way into the panelled library where he had lit the log fire half an hour previously.

"What will you have?"

"Whisky and water if I may. 'White Heather' if you've got it."

"Poor Andrew's brand. May I ask what has brought you here so urgently? I cannot imagine you would want to discuss Blenders just after this dreadful news."

Tim ignored the rebuke and said gravely, "I would not dream of foisting myself on anyone to talk business in such tragic circumstances, particularly when I am somebody else's guest. But there's more to all this than just business: it seems that Andrew's death was no accident."

"No accident? What do you mean?"

"There can be little doubt that this was deliberate. Andrew was the victim of a cunning murder."

Tim then summarised Frank's account of events.

James was appalled. "Andrew was one of the decentest men I know. He couldn't have been murdered. It's unthinkable. I've never heard a word said against him; he just didn't have any enemies."

"Maybe not," said Tim coolly, "but he did have a crucial 10 per cent of Blenders which was pledged to me."

"You can't believe he was murdered for his share stake. People just don't behave like that."

"Maybe your clients don't," countered Tim Weston, "but they're wealthy already. I can remember some suicides in recent years of City people who got it wrong. And in this case there are other bigger issues involved. A major Japanese corporation sees its very existence threatened if it loses an essential raw material. I've already had a brush with Sonkay and, although we didn't discuss the contract, it was clear that we would not be allies. And then you have a tough, and probably rough, American operator with a fortune coming to him on a plate. Those sort of people don't play by the rules of the Takeover Panel. The one thing that is certain is that I didn't want Andrew dead: our option on his shares was good only for his lifetime."

"Yes, I was aware of that," said James blandly.

"Then maybe you know also what becomes of his shares now." Weston's voice failed to conceal the raw urgency in the question.

James was taken aback by the callous intensity. "As it happens, I am an executor of Andrew's will. On the other hand, I have no idea of the liabilities. Does he still owe Forde Jamieson money, for instance?"

Tim shook his head. "He took out a huge term assurance policy to cover the loan – the insurance company is not going to like it much, but it was all properly done. On the other hand, will there be Capital Transfer Tax to pay on the shares?"

James nodded. "As you were his banker, I suppose you are entitled to know that there will be. He said he was going to take out policies to cover that later once Bormona was straightened out. His main assets were Bormona, his Blenders shares and his houses. Bormona and the houses go to

Marina, so there is no Transfer Tax there. But the Blenders' shares, all £30 million of them, go to Sarah – which means I suppose that something like three-quarters will have to be sold to meet a tax bill of nearly £23 million. I must say, after nearly forty years of inefficient socialism I find it more iniquitous than ever that people have to sacrifice capital to pay the wage bills for an army of civil servants who spend half their time administering each other." If James had a weakness, it was a habit of dilating on the uncheckable growth of the bureaucracy.

"Even though your firm has grown fat on the commission of private individuals who have to sell out to the institutions." Tim took advantage of his host's self-indulgence to launch a half-jibe.

James chose to deflect it: "A market of individuals is healthier. You get more people prepared to take unconventional views. But this is not the time to discuss market theory." Moving towards the decanter, he said, "May I freshen your glass?"

Sensing his welcome ebbing, Tim said swiftly, "Thank you, no, I must be going. But before I go, may I make a suggestion? As an executor, would you let me have an option on any shares you will have to sell?"

James stiffened: "One option of yours on those shares may have cost poor Andrew his life. Apart from the fact that it would, in a business sense, be extremely improper, I cannot think of anything in worse taste and more calculated to cause Andrew's family the maximum distress. Let me show you out."

James led the way thoughtfully to the front door; he was back inside the house before Weston was in his car.

"Not a very satisfactory person," was his summing up to Clarissa as he recounted their meeting over their lunch of salad, omelette and a half bottle of Macon blanc – both watched the scales carefully. "I can see why he has been so successful though. He's obsessed by business. He's shrewd, he's presentable, but underneath he's utterly ruthless."

"To the point of murder?" Clarissa saw events dramatically.

"I doubt it. I think he would draw a line at murder. In this case, anyhow, it was in his interest that Andrew should stay alive. The question is in whose interest was it that Andrew should die before Weston got his shares?"

"It must be the Japanese. They're quite ruthless, and didn't you say the killer was an Oriental?" With Clarissa's taste for drama went a preference for simple solutions.

"I'm not so sure. Killing for business reasons is not in the modern Japanese character and as everything has to be discussed at length, it would probably have to go to a board meeting. I just can't see them solemnly minuting it. It's really more what you expect of the Mafiosi. Using an Oriental as the hit-man might be a clever decoy." This speculation was interrupted by Pang, who, impatient for his customary tit-bits, commenced a staccato series of growling yaps. When the beast was finally mollified with some Ryvita, James abandoned the subject of Andrew's murder saying, "Well, we're not going to solve it now and I'm sure it's going to dominate the next few weeks. The clouds are coming up and if we don't take our proper dogs out for a walk soon it will be too late."

Frank borrowed one of the hotel cars to drive Sarah to Nice for the evening plane to London. Corkscrewing down the narrow looping roads, he kept well away from the valley side, hugging the mountainside with uncharacteristic caution whenever possible. Sarah's nerves were taut as reaction to the shock set in and although Frank knew the killer had already left France, he still felt a menace never previously experienced in the mountains. He had volunteered to stay in Nice to complete the formalities for the return of Andrew's body to Scotland and at the same time hoped that Inspector Jummel might get more leads from Italy on the killer. The mild winter sunshine at the airport and the hope of Spring in the air failed to lighten their spirits. Frank kissed Sarah tenderly at the barrier, saying, "Look after your mother: she needs you."

"And I need you, Frank," said Sarah simply as she turned and went through to the departure lounge.

Frank had booked into the Negresco: once ensconced in its *fin de siècle* comfort he telephoned the Inspector from his room overlooking the Mediterranean.

"We may have news, Monsieur Higgins, we may have news. They only remember one Oriental with skis at Milan airport yesterday – they are fortunately still rare enough to be memorable. He took the Alitalia flight to Rome, but he checked his luggage through to Beirut."

"Beirut, by God, that's strange."

"Truly, Monsieur Higgins. Orientals with skis are strange enough, but to live also in a battle zone, that is an extraordinary thing."

"Maybe – and maybe not. After all, a terrorist would feel at home there and I don't think you'd get very far with an extradition warrant."

"True, Monsieur Higgins. But we have our friends there too."

"Inspector, how quickly do you think it would be possible to make an Identikit drawing of the killer?"

"With top priority, by Monday. But what is the hurry: I cannot go to Beirut."

"No, Inspector, but I can."

Blessing the advantage of international dialling, Frank got through again to Tim Weston in Oxfordshire.

"Tim, I think I am on the track of Andrew's killer."

"What of it? We didn't do it. And we're not bloody policemen. Let them get on with it."

This callousness jolted Frank, who had come to accept Tim Weston's public face of the clever operator to whom money was just an enjoyable game of skill and nerve. The greed for power under the mask was now plain and stark.

Frank persisted. For him the hunt had become the opportunity to redeem himself in Sarah's eyes for the deceptions over Andrew's shares: in addition he was beginning to find the chase itself exciting. He carefully couched his arguments in terms of Forde Jamieson's advantage: "It must be significant that the killer is an Oriental. If we could pin this on the Japanese, no one in the City would have anything to do with their bid and it would leave the field clear for us. But the French police are powerless: unless we go to Beirut ourselves, no one will."

"All right," Tim was still reluctant, "but for God's sake don't get yourself blown up. Now, you're going to need all the help you can get. There are still banking families in Beirut. Before you joined us we used to have a lot to do with the Habib brothers in the days when the Gulf sheikhs kept their money in Beirut and it looked set to be the Geneva of the Middle East. The Habibs survive – they've been there for generations and like good bankers have a foot in every camp. I'll telex their number through to you in the morning."

As Frank set forth to see what Nice's bookshops could offer on the embattled Lebanon he reflected, "I suppose that's one meaning of good City connections."

That evening, Tim telephoned another of his connections. "Is that you, Robin? What did he say?"

"Well, I haven't put it directly yet. I just said that a friend of mine might want his backing and that it wouldn't cost him anything. After all, I don't know much about business myself."

"You'd better learn. What did he say when you told him your age?"

"Jumped. He didn't like that bit. How do you think I should play it now?"

"Is he in love with you?"

"Of course. To tell the truth I'm quite fond of him myself."

"You're supposed to be an actor. Play up to him. Say you've been reading all the stuff in the papers about Blenders. You'd like to stay with him but you'd feel much more secure if he accepted the bid – you like the thought of cash rather than shares which might be worth nothing."

"And if that doesn't work?"

"That's up to you. Have you any photographs?"

"I think there may be."

"Well then, use them. The deal is simple enough. When we get Luke's shares, you're cast as Bassanio in the Young Actor Company's *Merchant of Venice* which we are sponsoring. It's up to you to create your opportunity."

Replacing the receiver, Tim chuckled to himself, "Anyhow, it wouldn't be a bad bit of type-casting."

CHAPTER XIII

Marina and Sarah, sombrely splendid in black, arrived at Braithwaites' London office punctually for a ten o'clock appointment with James on Monday. Marina's raven hair and Byzantine features evoked Mediterranean grief, at odd variance with Braithwaites' Georgian furniture and pastel walls, embodying the pale spirit of Northern rationalism. James, who came to meet them, thought, God, she's magnificent, but these surroundings are wrong. Out loud he said, "We're all shocked at Andrew's death. Please accept the deepest sympathy from Clarissa and me. I'm sorry to have to ask you to come here: normally, of course, I wouldn't dream of talking about money yet, but this wretched bid business could be at a crucial stage. That's why I asked Lord Glencorres to come along also."

The courteous old peer rose as they entered, offering murmured sympathies.

Once seated at the mahogany conference table, Marina unexpectedly took the initiative. "Andrew will be buried at Lammermuir. It was his home and he loved it. Frank Higgins, who was with Sarah and Andrew in Bormona, is arranging for the return of his body. I shall let you know the funeral date soon. Now, James, what is there that we must talk about so urgently? I know all about Andrew's will: we discussed it together."

Realising her self-possession was a mask for grief rather than an expression of callousness, James began gently, "As you know, I am the chief executor of Andrew's will and responsible for sorting out his affairs. Normally, this has a slow momentum of its own, but the battle for Blenders means that important decisions may have to be taken quickly and as, between you, you are the main beneficiaries, I want to be able to take your wishes into account." He paused and looked kindly over his half-spectacles at the two women. "I must also explain that because of the way Capital Transfer Tax operates, our freedom of manoeuvre may be limited.

"Basically you, Marina, inherit Bormona and the houses while Sarah gets the Blenders' shares. As Andrew had wisely taken out a life assurance to cover his borrowings on Bormona, it comes to you, Marina, with enough cash to complete it free of borrowings, and as there is no Capital Transfer Tax between husband and wife, with nothing owing to the Revenue.

"Sarah's case is, unfortunately, very different and far from simple. In the first place, there will be Capital Transfer Tax to be paid, which on a sum this size will effectively be at a rate of 75 per cent. Andrew told me that he intended to take out a life assurance to cover the tax liability on his Blenders' shares as soon as Bormona was financially in the clear, but sadly he did not live long enough.

"As a result, Sarah, you have no alternative but to sell shares in order to meet the tax bill. Taking 300p a share, the price on the day Andrew died, his 10 million shares were worth £30 million. Ignoring any other assets for the moment, the transfer tax on this works out between £22 million and £23 million. Personally, I regard this as confiscation, not taxation, but sadly there is nothing I can do about it.

"The one concession the Revenue makes is that if you sell the shares, at any time within the next twelve months, tax is based on the actual selling price rather than the quotation on the day of death. In practice, of course, negotiations with the Revenue on an estate this size are liable to drag on for years, but as far as the shares are concerned, we must act within the year. Otherwise, if the bid for Blenders fails and the price drops back to 150p, probably about the right level, you could be left at the end of the day with shares worth £15 million and face a tax bill of £22 million. In other words, you would be bankrupt."

"But that would be monstrously unfair," put in Marina.

"Of course it would be, but unfortunately we are dealing with the raising of revenue, not the dispensing of justice. Why else do you think people emigrate to die abroad, rather than staying here, which they would prefer?

"But to get back to the shares, as you will have to sell three-quarters of the holding, you must also consider the other quarter, which amounts to 2½ per cent of Blenders. This is not a strategic holding and, as you don't work in Blenders, you must think seriously whether you want all your money tied up in what is, frankly, not a very successful company. Personally, I would take advantage of this bid to sell most of the balance at what looks to me a very generous price."

"I can't decide about that just now, James, but I do see what you mean about the transfer tax and I will be guided by you. The only thing I do know is that whatever the cost the shares must not go to my father's killer. I would rather sell everything and be dragged through the bankruptcy court first." Sarah's vehemence was intense.

"I sympathise entirely with that," put in Lord Glencorres as James nodded agreement while saying, "Unfortunately, of course, we don't yet know the identity of Andrew's murderer."

"We know who didn't kill him," said Sarah. "Tim Weston very much wanted Daddy to stay alive, so, I suppose, it would be safe to sell to him."

"The Japanese may appear prime suspects at the moment," said James, "but I am far from certain in my own mind. There are a lot of tangled motives in this business and I am unwilling to prejudge it.

"You will appreciate also that, as Braithwaites is Blenders' broker, I am liable to find myself in an awkward position. On the one hand, the company doesn't want Andrew's shares to go to an outsider, on the other in Sarah's best interests the shares may have to be sold around this price, which I'm afraid doesn't help Blenders. The company is not allowed to buy its own shares, the other directors can't afford to and even the tamest institution would jib at today's price if there were no prospect of a bid. In a way, it seems that Andrew's death makes a takeover bid all the more probable: certainly the odds are getting shorter."

Marina sat back, brooding, her fingers resting on the edge of the table. She spoke in a dry, harsh voice. "If the thing of which we are certain is that it wasn't Forde Jamieson and the shares have to be sold, then, James, we can't object to their having the shares. Furthermore, I would back Tim Weston to sort out that cretin Dougal Fordson. If he hadn't made such a mess of things my poor Andrew might still be alive. Now you know how we think, the decisions are up to you."

"You may remember, James," put in Lord Glencorres, "that last week we arranged a meeting with Mr Seizo of Sonkay here at noon. While I obviously don't expect him to admit anything, we might just possibly get a better idea of Sonkay's involvement after seeing him."

As Marina had lapsed into silent gloom, Sarah stood up, saying, "Thank you both for asking us to come here today. So long as Daddy's killers don't get the shares, we leave it to you, James."

"There is always, of course, the alternative of selling Bormona to raise money." James put the question in the form of a statement.

"I believe," said Sarah firmly, "that in spite of his Scottish pride my father would rather be remembered for Bormona, which was his achievement, than as a shareholder in Blenders. We'll sell the shares, James, to pay the tax man."

* * *

Mr Seizo, flanked as always by Mr Kaburagi and two silent aides, arrived punctually at twelve. As befitted his status, he was shown straight to the principal meeting room, where the Chippendale chairs were genuine and the portraits on the walls of the partners' ancestors. When James and Lord Glencorres arrived, Mr Seizo bowed and said, "We have just learned the sad news of the death of Mr MacLintock. Please accept our sympathy. I am deeply shocked."

"And surprised, too?" The old diplomat knew the value of shock questions.

The Japanese blinked, thinking he had misunderstood. "An accident in the mountains must always be a surprise: an avalanche can scarcely be expected."

"But it can be deliberately caused."

"Deliberately caused? Please explain."

"We have reason to believe the avalanche was started deliberately in order to kill Mr MacLintock."

"I must accept what you say," Mr Seizo spoke gravely. "It is very terrible. Who do you believe could be responsible?"

"As yet we have no idea." Prevarication was another professional skill Lord Glencorres maintained in his retirement.

"What motive could there be? Perhaps a local enemy?"

"Or someone who wanted to prevent Andrew MacLintock's shares in Blenders going to Forde Jamieson."

"I fail to understand." The Japanese looked genuinely bewildered. "How could his death affect his shareholding?"

"It was part of a complicated transaction which is now largely irrelevant." James entered the dialogue seeing that if Mr Seizo were, improbably, involved in Andrew's death, he was not going to be startled into an admission.

"Andrew MacLintock's death is a great tragedy for us and his family," Lord Glencorres continued sombrely, "but I know that he would have wished us to continue our efforts to ensure Blenders' independence."

"I am sure of that, too." The Japanese was clearly relieved

to be on more familiar ground. "It is our earnest wish also that you retain that independence."

"But you have been buying shares in the market."

"Quite so. We think you need help and support. We know you are not allowed to buy your own shares: you need friends to do it for you. We, in our turn, may need your friendship in the future."

The unmistakable reference to the renewal of the malt contract signalled the price of friendship.

Lord Glencorres returned to his frontal assault technique, "How many shares in Blenders do you intend to buy?"

The Sonkay chairman smiled blandly, "I understand we can buy 29.9 per cent without having to bid. We should certainly not exceed that amount."

James put in, "How do you propose to use your shares?"

"You can be assured that we would support the policies of the Board. We do not approve of takeover battles in the stock market – and we sympathise with the cause of your difficulties for we understand the risks in entering new export markets. Better perhaps than the financiers," he flashed what those ignorant of Japanese restraint might have taken for a hint of a grin at James, "and we know, too, the reward to be reaped once market share has been won."

Lord Glencorres was not to be deflected by general statements. "May I ask how you view the bid from Forde Jamieson?"

"Mr Weston invited us to a meeting: it was not helpful. We are prepared to support the Board and be permanent investors in Blenders. It is a concept we understand well."

"Would you expect a seat on the Board?"

"An invitation would indeed be appreciated. It could make it easier for us to discuss how we could help you with your marketing in Japan."

"That is not something on which I can make a commitment now: it would have to be discussed by the whole Board."

"Whatever you decide you can be sure of our support."

And with many expressions of mutual esteem, Mr Seizo and his party left, escorted to the front door by Lord Glencorres and James.

As they were driven away sedately in Monawa's black Rolls Royce – MON 1 – James said, "I know their history shows them to be ruthless but I simply cannot believe those careful, courteous people would conspire to murder Andrew."

"Even if the survival of their company were at stake?" Long experience at deception had left Glencorres cynical of the worth of appearances.

"Even then," replied James, who still trusted his intuitions.

Braithwaites' own deep discretion and sure belief in its inviolability leads it to regard elaborate formal security as not only unnecessary but perhaps a little vulgar. A younger and less self-confident house would have ushered such sensitive guests as Mr Seizo and his party anonymously out of the side door which in this case would have been proved wiser. An inconspicuous *Evening Star* photographer caught the handshake between the Chairman of Blenders and Sonkay: the City Editor got the story on to the front page under the heading "Japanese Reinforcements For Blenders". It was fuel for the gamblers in the stock market, where rumour and gossip quickly distil heady fantasies of profit. As the knowing reassured each other in discreet voices, "The Japs are about to bid at 400p a share: Braithwaites have it all sewn up", eager buying pushed the price up steadily. By mid-afternoon it was 375p.

"It was perhaps a little careless of us," observed James to Milo with a twinkle, "but it has done us no great harm. Now we must stir things up with Forde Jamieson's own shareholders. There's nothing as off-putting when you're wondering whether to pay up in a bid as the knowledge that your own shareholders are not at all keen that you should do so. Weston can't possibly afford to pay the present price – he was straining his balance sheet as it was. Now no one will be interested and his 280p has been left a long way behind."

"Even though we think without a bid the shares are worth only 100p on the profit outlook?" Milo still clung to facts as an anchor when the market's tides were running strongly against him.

"That outlook is essentially short-term: now that the market sees the value of Blenders to a bidder, the price will reflect that underlying worth also." Further mischief sparked in James's eyes, "Should we run the price up a bit further or try to dampen things down?"

"If the Japs aren't going to bid and Weston can't afford to pay up, is it wise to let the price get too far ahead?"

"The cautious voice of youth is very important in this business. You are right, Milo, and if things got out of hand, the institutions would be tempted to unload. Nevertheless, I think the price has got a little further to go – the market usually overdoes things. And as I am the executor of your uncle's estate we must be poised to make a start on that appalling tax bill. The more we can get away around this price, the better for Sarah."

"What about Sarah saying she didn't want the killers to have the shares?"

"I am somehow convinced that Sonkay are not responsible. And as the only other buyers appear to be the speculators, I have a clear enough conscience."

James's belief was not shared by Tim Weston. Speaking urgently that evening from his office to Frank who was still in Nice, he urged, "Get on with tracking down that Jap. If we can prove they are behind Andrew's death we can still pull this one off. Braithwaites have been cunning. They're using the press brilliantly – there's no one as unscrupulous as the Establishment in a corner. They have conned the *Evening Star* into believing in a Sonkay bid and pushed the price way beyond our limit. But if it does turn out to be the Japs who are responsible for Andrew's death, it will discredit Braithwaites too – it's about time they were knocked off their high horse."

"Planes to Beirut are not easy to organise – especially from Nice," protested Frank. "I am just completing the arrangements for the return of Andrew's body to Scotland and I'm waiting for an identikit drawing of the killer which I have been promised by this evening. I shall be in Beirut on Wednesday morning, the day after tomorrow."

CHAPTER XIV

"James, it's Luke Grey. I can see from the papers you have your hands full but there's something I'd like very much to have a word with you about, if you can spare a minute. Could we meet in Boodle's at about 6.30 this evening?"

Settled with drinks in their leather armchairs by the fire, Luke listened attentively while James narrated the day's events, then said, "To murder you can add blackmail."

"What do you mean?"

"For obvious reasons I always keep my private life very separate from my business life. Now, they're getting mixed up and I am being pressurised to accept the Forde Jamieson offer for my shares."

"By a young man?"

"Too young, unfortunately. He's under age. They're very hot at West End Central on sex with the under twenty-ones just now and I don't much fancy an appearance in court. Nobody minds if you are gay these days but they do mind if you vanish from society for six months – which was what Henry Cartwright got for a seventeen-year-old recently. I haven't had the full pressure yet but the scheming little bugger – although I must admit he's very attractive and I've let myself become fond of him – says he loves me and wants me to have the security of cash rather than shares in a company which he has read is going bankrupt. All a blind, of course, but he was careful to let slip how he treasured some rather indelicate photographs of us that got taken at a party."

"That's awkward."

"You must see it from my point of view, James. I want to stick by my colleagues on the Board – but I am not prepared to be a martyr for them. There's a long haul for Blenders on its own and success in the end is by no means certain. It's jolly tempting either to sell in the market at today's absurd price or at least take Weston's bid. After all, I'd probably keep my job and I would be a very rich man."

"Tell me about the young man. What is his name? What does he do?"

"Robin Jones. He's an aspiring actor. Did well at drama school – but like so many, can't get started."

"Is he devoted to the stage?"

"I think totally. It's the only thing he really loves, that inspires him. To tell the truth, it's one of the reasons I'm so fond of him. Unlike most of the other little numbers around, there is something genuine there."

"Luke, don't do anything about this for a couple of days. Stall the young man and let me work on something. But now I must be off. We are dining a very serious-minded pension fund manager from the North tonight, and his even more boring wife. Clarissa, as you can imagine, is not very enthusiastic. If I don't get home before they arrive, she is quite capable of going out and leaving me to look after them on my own."

As James came through the door of his tall St Leonard's Terrace house, with the lights from the standard lamps shining through the long Georgian windows of the first-floor drawing room, Clarissa called out, "They phoned to say their train had been delayed, thank God. That means we can have a drink in peace. I've been hearing about Blenders on the news and I want to know everything that's going on.

Normally you get all worked up about nothing at Braithwaites, but this time it sounds really exciting."

"I'll tell you while I'm having a bath. Be a darling and run it for me while I make a quick call."

James dialled the MacLintock number. "Sarah – thank goodness it's you, I didn't want to disturb your mother. Could you possibly ask your boss Leo Hudson to come and see me tomorrow? It's urgent and it's confidential. I don't doubt that he has lots of appointments but I feel he'll make the time. Just let me know first thing when to expect him. God bless you." And James replaced the telephone as Clarissa called, "If you don't come and have your bath now, I shall let the water out."

On Tuesday morning Leo Hudson arrived at Braithwaites promptly at 10.30 – as Sarah was still away a junior secretary had spent a frenzied hour re-shuffling his appointments. In spite of a fondness for the pleasures of the table he had retained a spare and upright figure. He affected an over-elegant appearance and time spent in the gymnasium and sauna was evident in the taut pinkness of his cheeks. His manner was aggressively charming, his conversation liberally sprinkled with celebrated names from politics and the media. In James's eyes at least these essentially negative characteristics were to some extent redeemed by Leo's quick mind and pleasure in getting to the heart of a problem.

"Gifted, but perhaps too overconfident," was James's immediate – and accurate – reaction. Leo Hudson's intelligence marked him out from the seedy pack of the City PR men, but the flashiness would always exclude him from the City's inner circle. His metier was the dirtily fought bid battle and Blenders, James reflected grimly, looked like being the nastiest he, James, had yet experienced. In addition, he needed Leo Hudson's access to the sleazier side of London and in return was prepared to give him the cachet of working for Braithwaites.

"How very kind of you to come at such short notice: I do appreciate it. I wanted to talk to you about Blenders and, as you will realise, there is no time to be lost. But first, may I ask whether you would be free to act for Blenders? You may well already have conflicting commitments."

Sarah had mentioned that she was doing some work for Forde Jamieson and James was partly testing out Leo Hudson's truthfulness. He knew that the temptation for Leo Hudson to switch loyalties would be immense. Appointment by Braithwaites and Blenders meant the recognition by the City Establishment which had so far eluded him. His decision was characteristically swift.

"We have been doing some work of a very general nature for Forde Jamieson, not connected with any specific bid of theirs. Provided we can agree terms, I should resign that account and there would be no conflict."

"That sounds fine. We know you're not cheap, but Blenders needs the best advice possible and I am sure you can give it. However, before we get down to the business of press conferences, advertising compaigns, letters to shareholders and so on, we have an urgent problem with one of our major shareholders where I thought it just possible that you might be able to think of a way to help."

James proceeded to outline the attempts to blackmail Luke. "I realise that this may seem rather an unorthodox request, but if you can think of any way to defuse this rather delicate matter, it would obviously be of the greatest assistance to Blenders. It's a bit outside our normal competence here, but it occurred to me you might be able to hit on something as you mix in so many different circles."

"How much would we be prepared to pay to buy off this young man?"

"I'm not sure it's entirely a question of money," said James. "According to Luke he is intensely ambitious to make a career in the theatre. If he is talented, it may be that we could do something. A number of our clients like to invest in shows: I can't say we encourage them, but if they enjoy being 'angels' that's up to them. And as they on occasion ask us to find propositions for them, there are a number of West End theatre managers and impresarios who owe us a good turn." James glanced at his watch, "There's an emergency meeting of the Blenders Board this afternoon and I'll get them to confirm your appointment. Meanwhile, this business of Luke's is the most urgent item on the agenda."

Back in his David Hicks office, an elated Leo Hudson summoned two of his partners to celebrate the new business with an early glass of champagne. "At last we are working for the 'blue-blooded' firms. And I can see now why Braithwaites stay at the top of the heap. There's James Murray looking like the chairman of the parish council, but he knows just how to deal with little blackmailers. He's thought it right through, but he's not going to dirty his hands himself. That's our job. The first thing is to get hold of young Robin. I have one or two possible leads, but if anybody else can come up with something, so much the better."

Faced with yet another board meeting that afternoon, Lord Glencorres declined James's lunch invitation and instead retreated to White's. As a refuge from the affairs of Blenders it was a total failure. Rumours that Andrew's death had not been an accident were beginning to circulate and Glencorres was soon surrounded by a mixture of concerned friends of Andrew's and those to whom it is an important aspect of self-esteem to know the true facts behind the rumours of the day. Most seemed ready to assume the Japanese were responsible. "Utterly ruthless . . ." "I remember them in the war . . ." "Don't let anything stand in their way . . ." "Just shows they can't succeed by playing fair . . ." Glencorres's mild rejoinder that Mr Seizo, whom he had met the previous day, appeared an improbable instigator of an ingenious and ruthless killing was politely regarded as a diplomatic evasion essential if, as the knowing assumed, Blenders was about to welcome a bid from Sonkay. On this topic, Glencorres maintained a chairmanly discretion.

The Blenders meeting, again at Braithwaites' offices, started sombrely. James recounted Sarah's story of Andrew's death. "Our *prima facie* suspect is the Oriental skier who hired the helicopter. He was, however, almost certainly an agent. We have no clue whatsoever as to the identity of the principal. The fact that the agent was an Oriental is no reason whatever for assuming that the principal was also."

"I wouldn't be so sure," interrupted a red-faced Dougal, "the Japs' motive is clear enough – they'll do anything to prevent Weston taking us over. I'd like to send some of my SAS friends in to sort them out."

"Be that as it may," said James tactfully, "I am told by Sarah that Frank Higgins is on the killer's track."

"Is he to be trusted?" put in Luke. "After all, Weston is deep in this whole business, too."

"Andrew's death was the last thing Tim Weston wanted," countered James, "and I think Frank is quite close to Sarah, so I am not too worried about his motives. As it's going to take the police a long time to report, anything Frank can come up with may be useful."

"Bloody waste of time if you ask me." Nobody *had* asked Dougal. "Amateurs nosing around, getting under the feet of the police. And I still wouldn't trust what he says – got too many of Weston's axes to grind. I still say it's better to see both of them off – Weston's crew and the murderous Japs. I could tell you some terrible tales about how they treated our prisoners of war in Burma – my uncle was there and barely survived."

"How would you see them off," enquired Luke acidly, "with your contract like a millstone around our corporate neck?"

"By doing the merger with Joseph Mabalian, of course, which I put to you last week. I agree it would make him the biggest shareholder, but that's better than being asset-stripped by Weston or absorbed by the bloody Nips and made to do press-ups to the company song every morning. Joseph is very keen still, even though the rise in the Blenders' price means that he would end up with less of the company. He's still in London and I think somebody should talk to him."

"We appear to have a fairly unenviable set of choices," observed Glencorres ruefully. "But I feel Dougal is right. However unpalatable, we must look more closely at Mr Mabalian's suggestion. James, you as our broker seem the most appropriate person to discuss matters with him and report back to the Board subsequently."

"Joseph is staying at Grosvenor House." Dougal was suddenly amiable.

"In that case," said James, "I'll go and see him there on my way home. Say at about 5.30: I don't want to be too late." He and Clarissa were invited to the English National Opera's new *Elektra* that night, expensively sponsored by a Braithwaite client. It was an odd process, in James's view, to use the profits of English capitalism to subsidise eccentric productions by East Germans who conscientiously put a Marxist gloss on even the heroic legends of the ancient world, but it had become an accepted part of corporate pomp – the modern equivalent of the mocking mediaeval jester.

Joseph Mabalian's suite in Grosvenor House was one of the more expensive ones looking over Hyde Park. The drinks trolley had been specially stocked with the brands Likkermart represented in America, typifying, thought James, the showmanship and thoroughness of the man who advanced to meet him.

He was broadly built, slightly less than medium height, bull-necked and with unusually large eyes. His dark, slightly wavy hair, with flecks of grey over the ear, and olive skin evidenced his Near-Eastern origins – part Greek, part Armenian, part Lebanese and, in practice, thought James, wholly Levantine.

As though to compensate for these slightly *outré* physical characteristics, his dress was excessively sober: dark suit, white shirt, plain tie, highly polished shoes. Although plump, he moved lightly: he spoke slowly, the East Coast inflexion and phraseology acquired at Business School overlaying an earlier more exotic accent and vocabulary.

"My dear Mr Murray, how kind of you to come and see me. Of course, I know well – he named the senior partners of two large New York broking houses, just below the front rank – and they have often spoken to me of you. I shall certainly tell them we have met. May I offer you a 'White Heather'? With water, I believe, and no ice."

"You have done your research well," said James guardedly.

"I always do." The wide grin displayed an unusual number of large, even, white teeth. The self-satisfaction was total.

"That's a very good deal you did with Blenders." James had learned early that businessmen are more susceptible to flattery than even the vainest of actors.

"It's been great for Likkermart stockholders, but it looks to be causing Blenders a few problems. That is one of the reasons I am here."

"I understand you have a proposition to put to the Blenders' shareholders," said James noncommittally.

"As I see it, Blenders makes the best whisky in the world and I've got the best distribution chain in its biggest market, so the companies are a natural fit. Just now I'm scoring a few points, but when the agreement runs out in a couple of years, I am going to lose that advantage. I certainly don't want Blenders to change control long-term just because of the good deal I've been fortunate to make short-term. I can't alter that deal – I have my own stockholders to consider – but I could put it to them that a merger with Blenders would enormously strengthen Likkermart's long-term potential."

James, who disliked being addressed like a public meeting, could not forbear the tart comment, "As I believe you own about two-thirds of the Likkermart shares, you shouldn't have a big job of persuasion."

Unabashed, his opponent countered smoothly, "That's a point, Mr Murray, that's a point."

"Braithwaites are, as you know," said James, "brokers to Blenders. Our recommendations will carry significant weight to shareholders: if we refuse to endorse a deal, it is much less likely to succeed. What is your proposition?"

"The price of Blenders seems to me to have gone a bit wild as a result of those goddam Japs getting in on the act. Maybe you could help here by letting the air out a bit."

"I'm afraid we're not very skilled at market-rigging," said James coolly.

"Well, that's a pity. But for our purposes now, let's work on a price of something over 300p for Blenders. Likkermart would issue 23 million shares at today's price of $25 in exchange for all of Blenders' shares and the deal would be recommended by the Blenders' Board. They would have solved their short-term problem and I would have strengthened my long-term position. It should all be very simple."

"As I am sure you are aware, Mr Mabalian, it is not nearly so clearcut. To start with, you are a relatively small company with only 5 million shares in issue. For most of last year they were trading on the over-the-counter market at between $5 and $7 – typical penny stocks. Clever financial promotion of your deal with Blenders had admittedly pushed the price up to $25 a share. But if you take over

Blenders, the combined company loses the currency advantages of that deal and I don't see why in those circumstances the shares shouldn't come back to below $10."

"You forget that they will be backed by Blenders' assets and longer-term prospects."

"Which you, in effect, will have bought for a song."

"Songs, Mr Murray, can be very valuable properties."

"The proposal is, I am afraid, too far-fetched. In terms of market capitalisation Blenders is about four times the size of Likkermart – and before the contract it was ten times. Likkermart is just a newish over-the-counter stock and a long way from Big Board status on Wall Street, while Blenders is one of our major, long-established companies. I can't see any circumstances in which we could recommend seriously any paper offer of yours, quite apart from the legal and other complications."

"That's what lawyers get paid for. But suppose the offer were underwritten for cash, so that Blenders' holders could take dollars if they didn't like our paper?"

"Who would underwrite it – we're talking of over half a billion dollars?"

"A group of investors in Colorado and Texas – Wall Street isn't the only money centre these days."

"I see, I see. But nothing is simple in England: our tax laws penalise taking cash in bids – it counts as a sale and is liable to Capital Gains Tax. What would happen to our holders of the new stock who stayed in?"

"We would go for a Big Board listing on Wall Street as soon as possible and then we could ask you to arrange a London listing for us."

"I still think it's a pretty doubtful starter, but, of course, I will consult with my colleagues. Now, if you will forgive me, I must leave."

"Don't take too long thinking." Beneath the surface jocularity was an implied threat.

"I'll be in touch before the end of the week. Meanwhile, we must both treat all this as highly confidential."

"You needn't worry. I'll say nothing to knock my stock price."

And James left, wondering why he so signally failed to warm to this shrewd man. Was it instinctive British mistrust of Middle Easterners – the original Wily Oriental Gentlemen – or was it something more fundamental?

And later in spite of Clarissa's threats to abandon the evening's opera if they didn't leave the house at once, James talked earnestly for five minutes to the senior partner of Chicago's most respected broking house.

CHAPTER XV

As the Middle East Airline's Wednesday 747 swung in over the great sprawl of refugee camps on the outskirts of West Beirut, Frank was profoundly thankful that a lull in the perennial hostilities left the airport open that day. The alternative of a flight to Damascus and a bumpy journey across the desert would have been exhausting in the stifling heat. Frank had known and enjoyed Beirut in the early seventies when its cool hills were the oil sheikhs' retreat from the burning summers of the Gulf and its bankers aspired to be the Swiss of the Arab world. The blend of Oriental, Mediterranean and French cultures under the hot sun had distilled a rare decadence – in his more fanciful moments Frank had claimed you could sense the corruption seeping through the paving stones. But it had been an elegant decadence: Frank regretted particularly the Hotel St George, a solid Edwardian Parisian establishment on the edge of the sea, whose cuisine and wine cellar combined with the azure setting to create a civilised paradise.

Gazing at the shimmering burnt-out shell of the city, Frank wondered what had become of the olive-skinned cosmopolitans who played backgammon daily by the gleaming poolside – probably they were by now in Monte Carlo, Florida, Singapore, London or New York, but certainly not enjoying as sweet a life as they had known here, destroyed pointlessly in a multi-sided civil war.

The few foreigners now stayed mostly on the outskirts of the city, relatively safe from the street shooting which erupted periodically in the old town. But Frank had booked in at the Grand, next to the burnt-out Holiday Inn in the old centre. If his quarry were, as he suspected, a professional killer, then his lair would be more easily camouflaged in an area where the pornography of violence was commonplace.

The taxi skirted craters and gun emplacements on the road in from the airport. At the sandbagged entrance to the hotel the doorman was still clad in the bright remnants of what an earlier management had hoped tourists would mistake for national costume. The lobby acknowledged more contemporary realities: a large table with typewriters signalled the workplace of itinerant journalists who periodically attempted to analyse the phenomenon of national suicide. The showcases for vanished luxury shops gathered dust: the one desk clerk worked by the light of a bare bulb.

The air conditioning no longer worked in the rooms and Frank was sweating as he dialled the number of the Brothers Habib. It took a war to expose the essential sinews of city life – water, electricity, sewerage, food deliveries, hospitals, telephones, taxis. The reason, it came home to Frank, that people risked their lives to maintain these mundane services was that, once they stop, a city dies.

A cautious voice answered the telephone. "May I speak to Pierre Habib?" asked Frank.

"M Pierre is not here."

"His brother Emil then?"

"This is Emil." The voice was cultured, the inflexion French.

"This is Frank Higgins. You may remember I had dealings with your bank here before the shooting began and now I am with Forde Jamieson in London. Timothy Weston asked me to give you his regards and, if I could come and see you, there is something which I would like your advice on."

"Ah, M Weston, indeed. You are in Beirut, M Higgins? *Mon Dieu*, that is brave. I should be delighted to see you.

Please, come and have lunch with me, we do not have many visitors these days."

The Habib villa, which was also the main office of the bank, stood on a rise looking out over the sparkling sea about half a mile from the hotel. When Frank had last seen the villa, it had been brilliant white, the gardens immaculate. Now the stucco was peeling, many windows were boarded up, the drive neglected and the gardens overgrown. Entering the banking hall, Frank was at first surprised to see a drab, patient queue depositing money, cashing cheques. Then it hit him that if a community is not to revert to the clumsy barbarism of barter, banking, too, is as essential as water or electricity.

An unshaven porter in a rumpled uniform fetched Emil Habib. In the surrounding seediness, the tall, thin frame in the neatly-pressed pale suit preserved something of the elegance Frank associated with the city. The long sallow face had aged terribly, the hair which Frank remembered as black was now grey, heavily streaked with white.

Once seated at the polished table in the cool, pale, high-ceilinged dining room, Emil said, "It is indeed a pleasure to see someone from London. At one time we saw many but this terrible senseless war has put an end to that. The Sheikhs keep their money in Geneva, London or New York now and we are back to providing a local banking system. We survive on it but it is not, as you say, any more the big time. But how can I be of assistance to you?"

"M Emil, it is an unconventional request. I need to contact a certain professional killer, a hired assassin, an Oriental, possibly Japanese, who lives, I believe, in Beirut, perhaps under cover of the PLO or the Japanese Red Army. I don't know his name: all I have is this identikit picture and the knowledge that he has just returned from Europe. How should I go about finding him?"

"Hmm. Striking features. May I ask your reasons?"

"They must be confidential. But if he were led to believe that I wanted to employ his services, that would be a harmless deception. And simply say I am from London. The company should not be mentioned."

"I see, I see. Beirut is full of killers. Some are just what you call gun-happy, some are sadists who kill for pleasure, some are fanatics who kill in the name of God or fatherland, sometimes both, and there are a few who kill for gain. I am happy to say I have no dealings with any of them, but I know they exist, and I know people who know them. Bankers, specially in the Middle East, live by their contacts and try to have them in every camp. Beirut is still a small city: if this man is here, there is a good chance we can find him. If you give me that picture, please, I will do what I can this afternoon and will call you in your hotel this evening.

"Now, tell me how is Mr Weston? I read that he has been very successful and that he is now established as a merchant banker." And lunch passed in the pleasant exchange of confidences, views, forecasts, reminiscences and assessments of personalities which are the staple fare of bankers' lunch tables everywhere.

Frank dozed fitfully in the hot hotel room between four and six: his half-world between sleep and consciousness was peopled with white-cloaked Arabs whose robes billowed open to disclose traditional Samurai armed with very contemporary machine-guns. He started awake and washed away the prickly sweat of heat and fear with a tepid shower. Waiting tensely for the telephone to ring he rehearsed again and again his story for the killer. To his analytical mind it sounded increasingly improbable with each rehearsal and the sweat of fear began to ooze afresh. Then, at last, the telephone pealed: "M Frank, it is Emil here. There is a person who resembles the picture you gave me and who has just returned to Beirut. He uses the name Itsuki Fujioka. I do not know him and I cannot be sure he is the person you seek, but a car will collect you in fifteen minutes to bring you to him. It has been a pleasure to meet you:

I pray circumstances will soon permit us more frequent visitors from London. Please give my kindest regards to M Weston."

The driver who collected Frank was swarthy, unshaven and unkempt, but his battered jeep ran sweetly. "Five minutes trip only," he said as they hooted their way through narrow arcaded streets, the blackened windows, like sad teeth stumps, evidence of the decay within. They stopped at a corner near the old souk and were met by an Arab youth in jeans and bulging combat jacket. "You go on foot," said the driver, "I wait." Frank's guide led the way through warm, spicy narrow alleys where the evidence of war was less oppressive, then abruptly into a courtyard lined with green plants, up a stone staircase to a heavy wooden door upon which he beat a rapid but definite sequence.

"Mr Higgins?" The Japanese who opened the door had the aquiline nose, hooded eyes, thin lips, strong chin and high forehead of the identikit image. He smiled, bowed courteously, and stood aside to let Frank in. Although dressed in a white burnous, Frank sensed at once the unusual strength and superb physical fitness of the compact frame. The furniture was cheap and nondescript. As Frank eyed it briefly, his host said, "You must forgive our surroundings: this is an apartment I borrow for meetings. My clients do not care to discuss business in public places and where I live in the hills, I keep private. Now, I am told you want to talk to me."

The youth in jeans was lolling in a chair by the door, a cocked sub-machine gun in his lap.

Salivating hard to ease the dryness in his mouth, Frank began: "I understand you may be able to help us. I represent a major international corporation and our efforts in Egypt are being frustrated by a certain individual who is, we suspect, in the pay of our competitors. It would be a great advantage to us if he were eliminated." Frank's throat tightened slightly and he started to sweat again as he came out with what sounded to him an improbable farrago. But to his host, it seemed to appear quite reasonable.

"Who is this individual, please?"

"He is a senior politician, a minister. When we have agreed terms, I shall give you the particulars."

"I see." The Japanese sat still, cold-eyed, tense. A fresh tremor of panic hit Frank's stomach. Would he be able to make any human contact with this impassive figure, trap him into an indiscretion about his last assignment? If his adversary suspected his real motives, another bullet-ridden corpse would attract little attention in this city of violent death.

Summoning his composure, he continued: "May I ask you some questions? We may have requirements in the future in other parts of the world and naturally we would prefer to limit the operatives we employ."

"I understand. I carry out assignments anywhere."

"Do you operate on your own or have you a team?"

"I am enough. I keep myself fit. I am a marksman, I ski, I climb mountains, I pilot planes, I operate underwater, I am an explosives expert. I am a team myself." This pride was the first crack in the facade: Frank attempted to widen it.

"Where did you learn these skills?"

"First in the Japanese army – the pathetic 'Defence Force' the Americans permit us which leaves my countrymen free to let their minds and bodies get soft. Then I was attached to your SAS in Britain. Those are men. Disciplined, dedicated to their fatherland." Frank, whose knowledge of the SAS was confined to his reading of the Sunday colour supplements, nodded mute agreement.

"So, Mr Higgins, you need not be worried about my ability – or my discretion. Let us talk fees. My basic fee is $500,000, plus expenses: one half payable in advance to my numbered account with the Credit Suisse in Zurich, the balance on completion."

The almost contemptuous tone in which the arrangements were detailed sparked the awareness in Frank that he was dealing with a fanatic, not a purely commercial killer. Sadist though he obviously was, some other motive moved him, and it was not money. Frank tried a barbed probe.

"With fees like that I can see why you left the Japanese army. The fatherland would never pay like that."

The yellow face tautened and the submerged menace was momentarily visible.

"I despise money. I love my country but it has betrayed me. It worships money, electronic trash, video recorders, not the ancient virtues I served."

The twisted idealism suddenly illuminated a name in the recesses of Frank's memory, Yukio Mishima, the post-war Japanese writer whose thinking fused aspects of fascism and Genet with a uniquely Japanese devotion to tradition. In vain protest against Japan's embrace of Western materialism and abandonment of her imperial tradition, he had literally disembowelled himself publicly in 1970.

Frank acted on the inspiration: "Did you know Yukio Mishima?"

The eyes of his opponent widened in sudden appreciation. "He was a hero, a true patriot. His death inspired me: it taught me that the Japan of today is not worthy of service. The money I earn will one day contribute to its overthrow and the return of a nation worthy of respect."

Frank sensed the possibility of a lead. "Would you then accept a commission from a Japanese corporation?"

"Never. Their enemies must be my allies. I will work for black, for white, for Jews, for Arabs, for communists, for capitalists, for oil-producers and oil-users, but for Japanese business, never, never."

Frank tensed himself for a high risk: "Have you ever had any contact with Sonkay?"

"They debauch my people with Western alcohol. I would like to kill all of them."

"Let us return to the reason for our meeting. We should much prefer this death to look like an accident."

"Understandably. I have studied the techniques: it is surprisingly often possible."

"This is most satisfactory. You will appreciate that I must talk now with my colleagues."

The Japanese stiffened. "I only deal with those fully empowered."

"Next time I shall be. How shall I contact you?"

"First I will expect the $250,000 deposited in this account," he passed a slip of paper to Frank. "You will waste your time until that is done. Then telephone this number and you will be collected. Ali," he barked to the young man in Arabic, who got up slowly and motioned Frank to go ahead of him, his gun still slung around his shoulder. Frank tensed, half awaiting a hail of bullets in his back, but once outside the building Ali concealed the gun under his battledress and led Frank, now trembling in reaction to the strain of the past hour, back to the waiting jeep.

CHAPTER XVI

Some diligent work amongst theatrical agents soon yielded Robin Jones's telephone number. When Leo Hudson got through on Wednesday morning the young man answered warily, but the hint of a possible part brought quick agreement to a drink in the Zanzibar that evening.

"It's lovely to be here, of course, but tell me, what is it in aid of?" Outwardly relaxed in the dark corner seat, rotating a glass of champagne, a perceptible edge crept into Robin's voice.

"A friend who saw some student productions at RADA said that you were brilliant and how sad it was you didn't seem able to land any work."

"Right on both counts. They made a special exception to let me in when I was sixteen and I worked my guts out when I was there. I even won one of their precious medals. But now the profession is so crowded I can't get so much as a walk-on part. As you might guess, I'm living on the dole – bloody waste of my talent and training. Because I am good. I know I'm good. I just must have a chance to prove it to others." The intensity took Leo Hudson aback. Luke's tale had led him to expect a more calculating, mercenary approach.

"Where do you come into this?" The tone was still cagey. "You say you're a PR man, I'm not much good at stunts, but tell me more."

"This is a serious acting proposition. I'm helping two friends, one with the Royal Shakespeare, one with the

National, to get together a company of young actors to tour universities in California with a repertory of English comedy – Restoration, Oscar Wilde, Noel Coward – and your name has come up as a possible. The plan includes a season at the Young Vic here afterwards. It's all under wraps still because they can't show their hands until they've put the company together. That's where I come in. When it's all set up they'll hand in their notice. The pay won't be great, but you'll get expenses and all the parts you can cope with. How does it sound to you?"

"Fantastic. Like a dream. Too good to be true."

"Well it is true. There's another thing. As the people involved are all in work at the moment and you are not, would you be able to go over straightaway, or at least as soon as you get your visa, and be the advance party? It would involve going to the universities, fixing up for the use of the theatres, organising advance publicity and so on."

Robin almost shivered in pleasurable anticipation.

"It's a double dream." Then doubt returned. "If the company isn't formed yet, how can I make the bookings?"

"Don't worry." Leo Hudson was at his most persuasively reassuring. "The company will be formed this week, and you'll have the names of the principals and two months' advance expenses before you leave. Now, are you free to do it?"

Robin hesitated, "There is something else I have been more or less promised, but it's not yet one hundred per cent sure. Just as soon as you tell me the company has been formed and who the principals are, I'll cry off the other thing – in some ways I'd be quite pleased to be able to. Now, let me get you a glass – this is something to celebrate."

After the third drink, when Leo suggested that they might go off and have dinner together, Robin was in a mood of happy acquiescence.

* * *

From his St James's flat the next morning, Thursday, Leo set to work on his favourite instrument – the telephone. With mock-modest elation he roused his acting friends: "I know it's early but it's important. I think I'm going to be able to arrange the sponsorship you need to form that company to tour California. There's one small string attached, actually I found him a rather agreeable one, by the name of Robin Jones. He's young, very attractive, did well at RADA and is desperate now to get some work. In addition, he would go ahead, organise theatres, do some publicity: I'll see to it that the sponsors cover the costs."

At 10 o'clock Leo went to see James Murray. "What I have to tell you is better not said on the telephone. Provided you can find a British sponsor for a tour of Californian universities by an outstanding company of young British actors in British comedies, Luke's problem will literally go away – about five thousand miles."

James chuckled appreciatively. "I call that a very positive solution. Now tell me, who would be the principal players and producers?" When Leo had told him, James lent back in his leather chair, cupped his chin in his hand and said reflectively, "I don't think this should present too much of a problem. Congratulations. Let me telephone this afternoon and confirm that all is well. And thank you very much for coming round."

After Leo Hudson had left, James put in a call to Sir Ron Pheasant at Commonwealth Tobacco.

"Ron, good morning. I hope business is going well. Good. Good. That's excellent news to hear. Now, Ron, I seem to remember you saying that you want to increase your market share on the West coast of America and that you need to create an elegant British image for your Gold Chip brand. Yes, I am sure it's going well but I am sure you want it to go even better.

"I know you like to stress Arts Sponsorship in your

marketing in this country and have been very helpful to some outstanding talents. Well, I have just heard of an opportunity to sponsor a first-class company of young actors who will be playing to young audiences in the Californian universities in just the sort of repertoire that would put over British elegance brilliantly."

That evening Robin rushed into Luke's flat. "The most fantastic thing has happened. I'm off to California next week for months and months and I'll be acting with a group of wonderful people. You're going to have to look after yourself for a while, my love, and you'll have to make up your own mind what to do with those lovely shares of yours. But don't forget me. Come and see me act out there. We could have lots of fun together."

"I'm sure we could," replied Luke with feeling. "Let's make a start now."

Later, after a considerable quantity of champagne, Robin phoned a Telemessage to Tim Weston at Forde Jamieson: "'Not happy in the part you cast me in and so must withdraw. My apologies.' What sort of card should it be? let me see. A condolence card – I think that would be appropriate."

At about the time Robin was dictating, slightly tipsily, to the operator, Frank arrived at Heathrow. Exhausted from a journey which had included a bumpy, stifling jeep ride across the desert to Damascus, for Beirut airport was again closed, and a long delay in Rome, his only thought was to call Sarah, to say he was safe and then to sleep deeply.

Refreshed, he went straight the next morning, Friday, to tell Tim of his Beirut meeting with Itsuki Fujioka. "So on the face of it," Frank was concluding, "it seems most unlikely that Sonkay were involved in Andrew's death – if they were, they have covered their tracks too well for us to

. . ." when he was interrupted by the delivery of a Telemessage.

"Twisting little sodomite." Blanched with fury, Tim crumpled the Post Office's sugary sympathy into a tight ball. "One day I'll fix him." Swiftly he regained his self-composure. He smiled formally at Frank: "Sorry about that. Something I had been counting on seems to have come unstuck." He paused for a moment, rose and began to pace up and down the carpet.

"Frank, you've done a first-class job in Beirut and you ran a considerable personal risk. I want both to congratulate and thank you: you can be sure the bank will show its appreciation in a practical way.

"But now we must assess where we stand on Blenders. What you have established, together with other developments here, puts our position in a fresh light. Frank, I don't believe any longer that we can get Blenders. The price has run away: I am far from sure that it's worth today's 360p a share to us, and even if it were we couldn't afford it. I've already had rumbling noises from some insurance companies which own our shares about the first price we offered. There would be an explosion if we upped the bid. The answer is we must sell our holding in Blenders, taking the profit on the shares. It won't do us any harm. We have 17 million bought at an average price of 260p: if we can sell them at today's price, the profit of £17 million will be very useful. It won't damage our reputation either. The market likes a management that knows its own mind and refuses to pay up. All in all, we might come out well from this – better in our pocket and in our pride.

"But it all depends, Frank, on our passing the parcel at today's price. Otherwise we could be hideously exposed, with a 17 per cent stake in a dud company for which we have paid too much. Remember ours is the only actual bid at the moment and I'm not at all sure that the Japanese want to buy Blenders. I think they might be quite comfortable with a 29 per cent holding – big enough to give them a say in

Blenders' affairs and to keep everyone else at bay."

"I am inclined to agree," Frank spoke thoughtfully. "To justify buying Blenders at this price you would have to undertake some major surgery. It might be all right for us to do it but I don't think the Japanese would risk the political unpopularity."

"Correct," Tim began to talk more briskly, fired by the relief of decision. "At the moment, they have declared a holding of about 12 per cent; our holding would fill them in nicely and bring them as close as dammit to 29 per cent. If we can do a deal with them at something like today's price, we're home. Once it's announced they've bought our holding and the bid's off, the price will plummet, so it's vital we maintain absolute security. If the market even suspected what we are up to, the price would start to slide and we could say good-bye to our profit. I'm afraid we'll have to keep our own fund managers in the dark this time. I suspect that more than one of them has a nicely anonymous Swiss bank account and the last thing we need is bears going short.

"I know you are only just back but I'm afraid the answer must be that you go to Tokyo and negotiate with Mr Seizo and his Board. Make the appointment and the travel arrangements from home: I'll say here you've got Middle–Eastern tummy and I have sent you away for a few days to recover. You've got full negotiating powers and unless it's very urgent don't get in touch until you have clinched the deal. And good luck."

Egged on by hints from the crime reporters that Andrew's death might not have been an accident, the City Editors of even the quality Sunday newspapers were proving ruthless all that week in their determination to splash the Blenders story. The Earl of Glencorres, through his charming, well-bred, wholly uncommunicative secretary, referred all calls to Leo Hudson. He in turn met every question with a routine, "The directors will not say anything until Forde

Jamieson issues its full bid document. They must study that first."

In the case of favoured journalists this was palliated with the promise of an exclusive interview the following week. But when the *Sunday Globe*'s analysis team threatened a two-page exposé based on hearsay and half facts, Leo undertook to give them some guidance.

On Friday morning Leo talked to James in one of Braithwaites' meeting rooms. Leo was adamant, "Unless we give them some sort of story they're bound to print a knocking piece on Blenders with a lot of painful innuendo about poor Andrew. The company has always been offhand with the financial press and this is just the opportunity they've been waiting for."

"What's our best line? There's not much we are in a position to say at the moment." James was not used to dealing with journalists in an aggressive mood – Braithwaites' relations with the press were mostly conducted with senior City Editors sitting over a lunch table to which they were flattered to be invited. He realised that he had never met an investigative reporter and decided that he was not anxious to.

"It depends on what you want to achieve. At this point of the game you must want to keep the Blenders' price up so that it stays well out of range of Forde Jamieson. The longer it holds up the less credibility they have."

"It's been slipping a little," conceded James. "It touched 380p earlier in the week, now it's back to 360p as the Japs seem to have gone quiet for the time being."

"We must stop it slipping."

"I agree but we haven't prepared our defence yet and we shall have our work cut out to justify a price of 300p let alone 400p."

"I shouldn't worry about that at this stage. This is a punters' market and we've got to appeal to their greed. Let them sniff another bid and the price will shoot over 400p."

"All right," said James. "Tell them I'll see them before

lunch on an off-the-record basis. All that I can truthfully say is that we are working on the defence, that the Japs have still to declare their position and that somebody else is possibly interested."

"Who?" Leo's voice was sharp.

"It's still vague – but nonetheless true," parried James. "And I'll admit that the police in France are investigating the circumstances of Andrew's death. How will that do?"

"If it doesn't put the shares over 400p on Monday, I'll retire to a lonely lighthouse," replied Leo satisfied that his reputation with the press would be, if anything, improved.

Back in the haven of the partners' room, James summoned Milo, "I think we should do something drastic about your cousin Sarah's Blenders. The price is getting terribly speculative and at the end of the day I cannot see that the company is worth 400p a share of anyone's money. The market price is not my responsibility but Sarah's wellbeing is. If we do nothing, the bid collapses and she still holds the shares in a year, she would end up penniless. What do you think?" The question was largely rhetorical, but James liked to rehearse his decisions out loud.

"It must be right," agreed Milo. "I should have thought that how we do it is more the problem. Forde Jamieson are out. If they pay more than 280p for a parcel they have to raise their bid to the higher price. And we know they can't afford that. We can't just sell the shares in the market either: if we let the jobbers sniff five or six million shares, knowing our relationship with Blenders they'd assume the bid was off and drop the price like a stone before we'd sold a single one. Even if we were prepared to place them with our institutions, the effect would be much the same. And what about the ethics of it? We are in a bid situation."

"We have no inside knowledge. And," retorted James, "Sarah has suffered enough in all this. We're not doing anything illegal and once I have safely placed Sarah's holding I will be happy to argue the small print of the takeover code for days on end with the old women in the Stock Exchange tower."

"All right," Milo was persistent, "but that doesn't solve the question of who is going to buy the shares."

"Look East, young man, look East." Decision had made James suddenly jaunty. Picking up the telephone he said to the operator, "Sally, my dear, ask Monawa for a number for Mr Seizo in Tokyo. I must call him while it is still a civilised hour with him." Turning to Milo, "I'm going to be tied up with the press until lunch and I want to get away promptly afterwards. Will you look after one thing for me? Telephone Mabalian and say that unfortunately it will be next week before we can give him any decision. Now, if I'm not in at the beginning of next week, say I've gone fishing. This is going to have to be a *very* discreet operation. Come to think of it, we can talk about it tomorrow: Clarissa and I are booked on the evening flight to Edinburgh for poor Andrew's funeral tomorrow. Will you be on the plane?"

"I'm afraid not, Marina is up there already and Sarah and I are going up in the early morning. The weather forecast is good so there shouldn't be any problem."

"Good, good. See you in Lammermuir, then."

CHAPTER XVII

Frank's only call from the immigration hall at Heathrow the previous night had been to Sarah. "I'm back. I've got lots to tell you. When shall we meet? I'm collapsing with tiredness and am scarcely coherent now."

"Come here tomorrow evening. Mother's in Scotland organising the funeral on Saturday. Are you planning to be there?"

"Of course I'll come."

"Good. We'll go together on the first flight on Saturday. There'll be quite a lot of other people on it as well but I'll organise a ticket for you."

They greeted each other with a long, passionate embrace. Disentangling herself, Sarah said, anxiously, "Do you know who killed my father?"

"Yes, but let's go inside and sit down: you give me a drink and I'll tell you everything that has happened since I left you in Nice."

When Frank had recounted his meeting with Itsuki Fujioka, he ended, "So we know who killed your father, but his identity is not important. He was only the instrument in the accidental shape of a human being – as far as I could see he has no humanity left, but has become a monster. I have no idea who programmed him, who is really responsible, but I feel reasonably certain it was not Sonkay unless they were prepared to risk using a non-

Japanese intermediary. I cannot see the Japanese entrusting anything so sensitive to a foreigner."

"If not the Japanese, then who, who Frank? Whenever I think about my father I feel so bleak and empty. I loved him so much, I don't know how I shall get through tomorrow. I can't bear funerals even of people I didn't know very well."

"Be brave, darling. I'll be with you then – and always if you'll have me."

"Always, Frank?"

"Yes, always."

"I want that." And they gripped each others' hands tightly to seal the compact.

"But, Frank, we must solve this business. Our best lead must be – who gained from Daddy's death."

"Let's work it out, who would have suffered most if our bid had succeeded?"

"Frank, that's it, that's it. I've been blind. Dougal Fordson. The first action of anyone who bought Blenders would be to get rid of him. Daddy told me that George Nunnelly, the finance director, said at the last meeting that the logical thing would be to put Dougal's company 'Mountain Mist' into liquidation. Blenders were too high-minded to consider it, but I can't think Forde Jamieson would be. Dougal's a bully, Frank, and I've always thought he was a thug. Frank, Frank, I remember him holding forth at a party about how marvellous the SAS are and about all the friends he had in it. That could be the link – you said that the Japanese in Beirut knew the SAS."

"He said that he was attached to them once."

"Frank, that's it, it was Dougal. How could he? How could he? Someone I've known all my life, someone who's been to this house, how could he?"

"I agree he is suspect, but we can't be sure."

"Well, I'm sure, Frank. You tackle him. He'll be at the funeral tomorrow, the brute. I don't know how he dares. All you need to say to him is that you have seen his friend Itsuki in Beirut. See how he reacts to that. He'll give himself away – I'm sure he will, I'm absolutely sure of it." And sobbing, she flung herself into Frank's arms.

"If he's guilty I'm sure he will, but now you must calm down. There is nothing more we can do at the moment."

"But you will tackle him tomorrow, you will, won't you?"

"Of course I will. Now, let me get you another drink, then we'll go out for something to eat, we've got an early start tomorrow."

Over dinner at the bustling Popote in nearby Walton Street, Sarah said, "You meant that, didn't you?"

"Meant what?"

"Always."

"Yes, actually, I did."

"Then I suppose we're engaged."

"I think that's what it's usually called."

"We can't tell people about it at this stage. Not with the funeral."

"Obviously not. I'm afraid I have to go abroad for a few days at the beginning of the week but after I get back I'll go to the jeweller's and then I must talk to your mother."

"Are you going abroad for the bank?"

"Who else?"

"Tell me about Tim Weston. Was he furious when he discovered he wasn't going to get Luke's shares either?"

"I never knew we were supposed to be getting them."

Sarah giggled, "I'm not surprised Tim didn't boast about it. It was rather the department of dirty tricks. I must say it had its funny side and Leo, who couldn't resist telling me how he pulled the strings, loved every minute."

Frank listened tight-lipped, then asked, "Did Luke's young man send Tim a condolence Telemessage?"

"I believe he did. It must have made Tim livid."

"It did. More seriously, darling, you must have realised that as I got to know you better, I became very unhappy at the tactics Tim was using to get your father's shares. Still they were just about legal, but blackmail is something else.

If this is to be the style I must think hard whether I want to carry on with Tim."

"That's something we can discuss another day. I love you very deeply, probably more than you realise, but tonight I must sleep on my own. So drop me home and be back at 6.30 in the morning. I'll give you breakfast before we head for the airport."

CHAPTER XVIII

Light clouds scudded across the low rounded Scottish hills, dappled in shades of grey: a watery sun shone through, too pallid to cast shadows from the leafless trees lining the narrow road between the MacLintock house and the village kirk. The ploughed fields on either side were still in the grip of winter: there was an almost total absence of living colour. Inside the grey stone kirk the scene was equally sombre. Mourners filled the dark brown pews while the coffin, draped in black at the head of the aisle, magnetised all eyes. Frank made a covert survey of the congregation. Among the relatives, friends and neighbours he recognised directors of Blenders, their faces familiar from the Annual Report. Otherwise the ranks of the mourners were largely anonymous. But when Sarah and he did, finally, get married, the same faces would return, this time in joyful clothes and the countryside would be lit with sunshine and colour.

The reverie gradually turned the service into a negative image of a wedding. The sermon on the life hereafter, united with Christ, became a parody of the standard homily on marital unity. The stately departure of the coffin, carried aloft by four soldiers from Andrew's Territorial Regiment, to a solemn march on the organ, swivelled the heads in each row just as does the exit of a bride going to her new life. Outside the kirk Frank joined the queue which filed past, not a smiling couple, but a mournful Marina and Sarah and a dark void in the earth. Even the murmured condolences were a macabre echo of murmured congratulations – "terribly sad", "terribly glad".

Back in the house, the illusion persisted. Admittedly there was whisky rather than champagne but once the initial restraint had thawed, voices rose steadily until within an hour the full-throated party roar was indistinguishable from the most raucous wedding reception.

Saying, "You must meet my godfather", Sarah brought Frank through the hot and noisy room to where James had just finished talking to Lord Glencorres. "Uncle James, I want you to meet Frank Higgins who was with us in Bormona. Now you must excuse me: Mother needs help with some of the old aunts."

James looked approvingly at Frank, "I understand that it's thanks to you that we know this tragedy was no accident. Your behaviour on that mountainside was both shrewd and brave: I admire you. Sarah tells me you think you may be on the trail of the killer: have you had any luck?"

"He'd do better to keep his nose out of our affairs and get out from under the feet of the police. If his bloody lot hadn't put their oar in in the first place, none of this would have happened." A flushed Dougal, whisky tumbler clenched in his coarse red fist, lurched between James and Frank, his bloodshot eyes signalling unguided aggression. "Think you're so bloody clever, don't you: quite the little James Bond. You City slickers make me sick: you've never had to deal with the real world of empty order books and full pay packets. You just sit there with a telephone shuffling bits of paper and think you're fucking clever. You're so sharp you'll cut yourselves one day – as you seem to have done here. Maybe you haven't though. The thing about you fellows is that you hardly know yourselves which way you're facing: it might suit your book to have Andrew dead and buried."

"Shut up, Dougal. You're being gratuitously offensive." James was taut with anger. "If you can't hold your drink, you'd better go and sober up."

The rebuke only stoked Dougal's ire. "You think you're so high and mighty, whiter than white, at Braithwaites, don't you, James, laying down the law, saying what we can do and what we can't do and what all your silly little codes and rules allow, putting in a word here, making an introduction there? But you've got to shuffle papers too, and take your 1 per cent each time or else you'd go hungry. You're not much better than him at the end of the day. What's he doing here anyhow?"

The volume of Dougal's voice rose in line with the wildness of his accusations and conversation in neighbouring groups dwindled into fascinated silence. His audience, feigning inattention, waited expectantly for the next outburst. Its extravagance did not disappoint them.

"I expect you're probably in this together. He's come up here to sniff around and try to buy poor Andrew's shares from Marina or the executors. At least he'll have to pay a bit more than under his first crooked scheme. I'm sure you'll find them for him, take a fat commission and charge Blenders a fee for advice on what to do at the same time. It's just as well . . ."

"I talked to your accomplice Itsuki Fujioka in Beirut this week." Frank decided the moment had come for brutal shock tactics.

Dougal paused, puzzled. "Itchy? Itchy who? What the hell are you talking about? I've never been in Beirut in my life. Stinking city, full of bloody wogs." Dougal's voice took on a note of sarcastic glee. "But you won't find any Blenders' shares there. They're here. And we're here. And we don't want you and your kind. So get back to your paper passing, Mr Higgins."

Lord Glencorres, who had quietly approached, spoke firmly: "Dougal, that's enough. There's something I should very much like to talk to you about." And gripping Dougal's elbow he steered him determinedly into the next room.

"That was embarrassing," Frank smiled wryly at James

who countered quickly, "What was that about an accomplice in Beirut?"

"Just a theory of mine – but it doesn't seem the right one."

"I'd still like very much to talk to you about Beirut."

"Willingly," said Frank, "but I see Sarah coming now."

She was confused and upset. "I know I asked you to tackle Dougal, Frank, but that scene was dreadful. Was there no other way?"

James moved quickly to Frank's aid. "The provocation was entirely on Dougal's part, Sarah, he'd had several glasses too many and became exceptionally offensive. Fortunately, Lord Glencorres was marvellous and employed his best Governor-General technique to get Dougal under control."

"But Frank did say something about Beirut?" Sarah persisted.

"With nil effect," said Frank, "he looked quite blank."

Clarissa quietly joined the group and hooked her arm firmly through James's saying, "Darling, unless we leave now, we shall miss our plane back."

"Straightaway, my dear, straightaway." Turning to Frank, James said, "Let's be in touch next week. I still want to hear all about the Middle East."

"James is quite right," Sarah spoke firmly. "This is not the time for solving mysteries. I want you now to come and help me cope with some of the great-aunts."

CHAPTER XIX

Bone-weary from the sixteen-hour flight, Frank checked in thankfully at Tokyo's busy, impersonal Palace Hotel the following Monday. But before resting he wanted to fix an early meeting with Sonkay: the need for security had ruled out advance arrangements. Normally a formality in the West, the task loomed daunting in the East and Frank felt suddenly helpless without secretaries and anxious-to-please stockbrokers making introductions, explanations and appointments, producing interpreters, organising cars and booking restaurants. This sense of helplessness was heightened by finding the Tokyo telephone book in his room printed entirely in Japanese script – one of the few indications that his characterless cell was not in Abu Dhabi or Dallas. Such minor hazards served to shroud Frank's real worry: would Sonkay actually want to buy Forde Jamieson's holding in Blenders? The one meeting in London had been unfriendly and Sonkay's motives and strategies remained enigmatic. If they didn't buy the shares then Forde Jamieson would have made its first major, public blunder. Success touches a deep-felt spring in the City's collective consciousness; like any small community at the mercy of apparently inexplicable and uncontrollable forces, it has a deep need for heroes able to outwit those forces. But always the crowd in the marketplace is waiting for the current hero to make a false step; at the moment of fallibility the admiration evaporates and the shares the fund managers boast of in the wine bars quickly become the ones nobody wants to admit owning. Frank was uncomfortably aware that if he failed with Sonkay, Forde Jamieson's days of glamour would end and he would join the ranks of the failed whizz kids.

Sonkay's Annual Report fortunately yielded a telephone number and Frank got through to Mr Seizo's secretary with surprisingly little difficulty.

"You say that although you met in London, Mr Seizo is not expecting you but that you would like to see him urgently. That may not be easy, Mr Higgins. He is in Osaka today, and will be in meetings tomorrow. Can you be so kind as to tell me what it is about? Blenders. I see. I think you should perhaps talk first to Mr Saginuma. I shall ask his secretary to contact you at your hotel: then if he thinks it appropriate a meeting could perhaps be arranged with Mr Seizo on Wednesday. What is your room number, Mr Higgins?"

The Sonkay Annual Report revealed that Mr Saginuma was the director in charge of overseas activities. Knowing that Japanese corporations always aim to build a consensus within the company for all major decisions, Frank realised that he would in any event need Mr Saginuma's support. When the telephone dutifully rang three minutes later, Frank told the secretary (who did not speak quite such fluent English as the chairman's) that he would be delighted to dine that evening, then fell gratefully on to the bed.

Punctually at seven the telephone rang, Mr Saginuma was in the bar. Frank would probably recognise him because he had been with Mr Seizo in London. He was in his thirties, slim, middling height, didn't wear glasses and would be holding a copy of the *Far Eastern Economic Review*. On meeting, he turned out to be also large-eyed, earnest and apparently lacking in anything an Occidental would recognise as a sense of humour. He bowed deeply, saying, "It is an honour to welcome our fellow shareholder in Blenders to Tokyo. I am sure we have much in common and many things to discuss about our future co-operation. But first let me buy you a glass of our 'Imperial' which, as you know, includes Blenders' malts. Then we shall dine at Tokyo's garden restaurant, The Happo-En, so that you can see something of our traditional Japanese way of life. Is this your first visit to Tokyo?"

Mr Saginuma boasted an MBA from Berkeley, which had veneered on to his traditional politeness volubility and an urge to keep control of the conversation. To Frank, still jet-lagged, this had the advantage of giving him the opportunity to work out Sonkay's priorities without showing his own hand. That, he suspected, should be reserved for the meeting with Mr Seizo.

The Happo-En, a wooden building in expensively manicured gardens, partitioned within by paper screens, turned out to be one of the last refuges of the geisha. Observing the wrinkled skins under the heavy, masking make-ups, Frank concluded that the occupation must be suffering from recruitment problems. But the novelty of having prettily prepared food virtually fed to him was soothing and the crones applauded dutifully when he downed a plate of tiny, wriggling fish in one nauseating gulp. Mr Saginuma meanwhile maintained a steady flow of information on Sonkay's history, the correlation between middle income and whisky consumption in Japan, the growth of Sonkay's market share and its export achievements.

Fighting back the mounting waves of tiredness, Frank essayed: "Your export marketing has been highly successful. I suppose you will apply the same techniques to Blenders."

His host stiffened slightly. "Excuse me, but I do not see how that could arise. We are shareholders in Blenders together. We are not managers. But naturally we should be very happy to help with advice."

"Do you believe the Board will listen to you?" Frank wanted now to crack the correct facade.

"We have, as you know, other relationships with Blenders. For instance, they supply us with the malt for our 'Imperial' blend."

"And you hope they will go on supplying you."

"Oh, I am confident they will. Is there not still a surplus of malt: I think you might even call it a malt lake. And are we not loyal shareholders?"

"Why did you think the supply would be in danger if Forde Jamieson got control of Blenders? We are highly commercial people."

"Of course you are. But if you will forgive me saying so," here a possibility of humour glinted in Mr Saginuma's eye, "you are also a wheeling and dealing conglomerate. If you get control of Blenders this year, you might not have it in two years' time? We are happier with the traditional management whose thinking we can understand and respect – but we are content to influence it, not to control it."

"Was that why you went to such lengths to knock us out?"

"What lengths, Mr Higgins? To be frank, we were not unduly concerned by your intervention. After all, we were able to see from your balance sheet that you would not be in a position to increase your bid. All we had to do was to buy enough shares in the market to keep the price above your bid: then it was bound to fail. Your bank, Mr Higgins, took a high risk when it tried to buy Blenders. If there had been no opposition, you might have succeeded. The shareholders probably would have sold it to you, but theirs are not the only loyalties to be considered. There are also workers, suppliers and customers. You didn't bid for them, Mr Higgins, and they have defeated you. We understand well these other loyalties in Japan – and fortunately we also understand how stock markets function."

Something more than the ghost of a smile was now playing round Mr Saginuma's lips. "There remains, of course, the question of what to do with your shares. Ah, I see our soup is coming."

The clear salty soup which normally concludes a Japanese

meal was served with full ceremonial reverence. Frank seized the opportunity to change conversational tack.

"Do you travel much in your business, Mr Saginuma?"

"Yes, indeed. I fear my family suffers from my absence, but my work demands it."

"The Middle East?"

"The alcohol business is delicate there, as you must know, but we have our agents."

"Is Itsuki Fujioka one of them?"

Mr Saginuma registered blank indifference. "I don't believe I know the name. Is he a contact of yours?"

"In a manner of speaking." Fortunately for Frank, the geishas were then encouraged to perform their party piece for visiting Anglo-Saxons – a scrawny and dimly recognisable version of Greensleeves on traditional instruments. This signalled the end of the meal and, shortly afterwards, with much bowing and smiling, Frank and Mr Saginuma were escorted to Sonkay's waiting black car.

"Tomorrow," said Mr Saginuma as they approached the hotel, "you should visit Kyoto for the day. I shall send a car to the hotel at 9 o'clock. The driver will bring you to the station and put you on the train. On Wednesday he will collect you at the same time and bring you to our offices for a meeting with Mr Seizo." Frank mustered his energies to thank his host appropriately, then went thoughtfully to bed.

Kyoto, the ancient capital of Japan, encrusted with precious palaces, shrines and temples, is the country's main tourist attraction: it draws over thirty-five million people a year. But in winter it is half-deserted, the fragile, brightly painted buildings crisp in the bright air, far removed from the smog which shrouds the main industrial cities.

Why, Frank wondered as he gazed thoughtfully at the impassive five hundred and fifty ton gilded Buddha in the Daibutsu-den, were Sonkay so anxious to send him to

Kyoto? Was it hospitality? Or did they want to keep him out of touch? A telephone call to Tim when he returned to the hotel that evening – it would be morning in London – seemed called for.

Responding dutifully to his guide's nudging, they returned to the car for Nijo Castle. It's really a cliché, thought Frank angrily, gazing at delicate golden screens of herons and cherry blossom, to contrast this refinement and delicacy with the brutality of which the Japanese are notoriously capable. I must be able to learn something here that will help me in my dealings with today's Japan. But the only clue came in the "nightingale floors" in the approach to the Shogun's apartment, which creak and groan at the lightest footfall to warn of approaching intruders. The Japanese, Frank realised, are not easily caught unawares. And they are geared to expect treachery.

Back in Tokyo, after three hours in the air-conditioned comfort of the bullet train, Frank experienced a sudden craving for robust, Western food – steaks, fried potatoes, even chocolate pudding. Remembering the coffee shop in the hotel basement he hurried in. As he looked around for a seat he saw James Murray eating at a table on his own in a far corner. James rose, shook hands, saying, "Well, this is a nice surprise. I was hoping to talk to you this week, but I never expected it to be in Tokyo."

"What brings you here?" asked Frank.

James side-stepped the question, "My Japanese hosts have invited me to dinner at the Happo-En. As it's more elegant than filling I thought it would be wise to take some calories on board first. Now, why don't you join me? It would give me great pleasure and also the opportunity to hear about Beirut."

"Thank you," replied Frank. A waitress came to the table: "I don't think I shall ever look a raw fish in the gills again. Minestrone, sirloin steak, French fried, spinach and a carafe of red wine. That should make me feel a human European again. Now, let me tell you about Beirut."

When Frank had finished his narrative, James said, "This makes the second time in a week that I have called you brave and shrewd: Sarah is a very lucky young woman."

"And I regard myself as a very fortunate man."

"Hmm. How fortunate depends on the outcome of my visit here. But that's another matter. You say the killer was Japanese?"

"Openly and obviously."

"But that he hated the Japanese business class."

"So he said. He could have been lying – but I don't see why he should."

"Quite. And there certainly are traditionalist fanatics in this country. He's probably genuine."

"So it's unlikely, then, that he would have worked for Sonkay."

"My dear Frank, they would never have hired him, or anyone like him. They are much too correct and they don't need to. They have brains and money and they know how to operate the market mechanism. No, it's the action of a desperate man who cannot afford to fight it out in the market."

"Dougal seemed to me to fit that bill," said Frank, "but you remember he looked genuinely blank when I tried the killer's name on him during that scene at the funeral."

"It wasn't the killer's name that set him off, was it?"

"No, he was well under way already."

"Yet," said James, "Dougal, Dougal. I think it might be the right track, even if it's not the right man. As we used to say in children's games, we're getting warm. I must think about this. Now tell me, how are you getting on with Sonkay?"

Frank flushed, "What makes you think I am here to see them?"

"Frank, who else would you be seeing? Forde Jamieson has no existing business in Japan and would scarcely send a key man in the Blenders' battle to scout for new clients at this juncture. You've come to talk to Sonkay. Now, let me try to work out why. You've lost Andrew's holding, you've lost Luke's – and I must say, I had not expected those sort of tactics from Tim Weston."

Frank, becoming more and more embarrassed, said, "Believe me, I knew absolutely nothing about that."

"I'm sure you didn't. It's very much the sort of thing someone like Weston would keep to himself. Be that as it may, you've lost Andrew's and Luke's holdings and you're left with the 15 per cent or so you've already bought. You're not doing badly with that holding, of course. The price touched 400p yesterday on the weekend press comment and although it's back to 380p now, it's still way above the price you paid and your bid of 280p. Your problem at Forde Jamieson is that you cannot afford to increase that bid in a worthwhile way because you're not big enough. So what do you do? You don't need a business degree to realise that the answer must be to take a profit on your holding while the price is high. But you can't sell it in the market because if the jobbers saw you coming, they'd know your bid was off and they'd drop the price like a stone. Who does that leave? Sonkay. Fill Sonkay in and your problem is solved. How have you got on with them so far?"

Frank said quietly, "James, this puts me in a very awkward position."

"More awkward than you perhaps realise. I am here for the same reason. Only the shares I am selling are Sarah's."

"Sarah's? I had no idea. Obviously I knew they were in the family but I assumed they were in trust or would go to Marina. I suppose, had you asked me, I would have expected her to be a long-term holder – like those directors' holdings which never change from year to year in the accounts and are a fixture, like the family house."

"Even family houses have to be sold sometimes to meet the taxman."

"Are you sure it's as bad as that?"

"I'm afraid so. Andrew died the day you announced your bid which meant that his 10 million shares, at the closing price of 300p, were worth some £30m: the CTT on that will be over £22 million.

"Sarah has no other assets to speak of, so she has no alternative. I advised her also to take advantage of the bid and sell the remainder of the holding: there seemed no point in hanging on to 2½ per cent of an inefficiently run company. She tells me, very privately, that you and she may become engaged. If I sell her shares to the Japanese now, at least she will have a handsome dowry."

"I don't give a damn about the money. It's Sarah I want to marry. I can support her. On the other hand, it would be doubly shocking if this whole affair were to deprive her not only of a father, but also of the bulk of her fortune."

"You put it very well," James spoke gravely. "Have you opened up to the Japs at all yet?"

"I spent yesterday evening fencing warily with Saginuma and I am supposed to see Seizo tomorrow. They packed me off to Kyoto today."

"Probably because it was my turn with Seizo this morning."

"How do you read them? Do they want the whole company?"

"I don't believe they do. They want to secure their malt supply and prevent anyone else gaining control of the company. They like the present style of management: it's not aggressively competitive. Something between 25 per cent and 29 per cent would give them Board representation and make the company bidproof. So far they have declared 12 per cent: that means that either Forde Jamieson's or Sarah's holding would suffice – they could always top up Sarah's in the market. Even if they were prepared to buy both they couldn't as that would put them well over 30 per cent and trigger a bid."

"What line did they take with you?" asked Frank.

"They have obviously read you as a seller, so they are going to try to play us off against each other. They were, of course, very polite when I saw them. They said, Yes, that at the right price they might be prepared to deal, but hinted that I was not the only seller and that for a large line they would probably not pay more than the 280p you had bid, but even that was not certain and they have invited me back tomorrow afternoon. Naturally, I should like to salvage as much as I can for Sarah."

James glanced at his watch, "Good Lord, Saginuma has been in the foyer for the last five minutes. I must go at once: it would upset things if they saw us together."

"The geishas play a remarkable Greensleeves: you should ask for it after dinner," Frank grinned mischievously.

CHAPTER XX

At 9.30 on Wednesday morning, Frank was seated in a low chair in Mr Seizo's simply furnished pastel-shaded office: from its twentieth-storey window the chequerboard of Tokyo's grey acres, two-storey houses nestling in the shadow of skyscrapers, stretched to the clear horizon. Once ritual tea had been served by two tiny elfin-pretty girls – a great improvement, in Frank's eyes, on the traditional blunt-faced British tea lady – he squared up to the polite but curious stares of Seizo, Saginuma and the company's finance director, who in traditional Japanese adversary ritual were ranged along the sofa opposite.

"We are very pleased to welcome you to Tokyo," said Mr Seizo blandly, "and honoured that you have come so far to talk to us. We take it that your presence here indicates your desire to join us in supporting the present Board of Blenders. This, I remember, was my proposal to you at our last meeting."

"I remember well, Mr Seizo. We, of course, respect your motives and understand the importance to you of the renewal of your malt contract. But unfortunately we cannot share your confidence in the present Board. If our shareholdings – your company's and mine – are not to diminish in value, then action must be taken to change control of the company. As I am sure you are aware, we are not in a position on our own to increase our bid. However, I am happy to say we have found a major partner in this enterprise and we are setting up a new, jointly-owned, company which will be in a position to make a bid of 380p a share for Blenders."

"This is most interesting." A quick, sidelong glance at a startled Saginuma was as close as the Sonkay chairman came to a reaction.

"What is the identity of your new partner?"

"I am afraid that must still be confidential at this point, but I can assure you it is an internationally known name. My reason for seeking this meeting is to ask whether you would be willing to participate in this new company which is to make the bid, on terms which would guarantee you your malt supply. Alternatively, would you be prepared to sell us your holding at 380p on the understanding that we would again provide you with that guarantee?"

Mr Seizo paused to confer briefly in Japanese with his finance director. "If we were to follow one of these courses and your bid were still to fail, what would happen to our malt supply then?"

"That would be up to the present Blenders board: I cannot say what their reaction would be. On the other hand, there is a large surplus of malt, they need all the revenue they can get, so I should be surprised if they refused to renew the contract. The question is, however, hypothetical as with your support we could easily win."

"Ah-ha. You would ah be prepared to take all our shares at this price?" asked the finance director.

"And more if you can find them." Frank spoke with aggressive buoyancy. "We shall not fail a second time."

"This is a new and very important development, Mr Higgins," replied Seizo. "You will appreciate that we must have discussions here before reaching any decision." Another brief conference in Japanese. "We thought you would perhaps be interested in saké making while you are here and we could arrange a tour for you this afternoon."

"That would be most kind." Frank politely feigned enthusiasm.

"Then Mr Saginuma will be in touch with you at your hotel this evening."

"I look forward to that. Thank you gentlemen." And bowing slightly as he shook hands, Frank was escorted by Mr Seizo's secretary to the Public Affairs Department for his tour.

When Frank returned to the hotel that evening from his initiation into the techniques of saké production, he telephoned James to meet him in the bar. James arrived, elated.

"I don't know what you said this morning, Frank, but it went like a dream this afternoon. Seizo suddenly grasped the technical problems of dealings in large lines well below the market price which he had dismissed yesterday. I sensed that they had turned buyers today and the upshot is that I have a banker's draft for Sarah's entire holding at 370p and instructions to buy another 5 per cent. It seems they already got 14 per cent of the company, and that would give them their 29 per cent."

James was interrupted by a high, "Mr Higgins, Mr Higgins, telephone." The pageboy led Frank to the lobby booth. "Mr Higgins, this is Saginuma speaking. I hope you enjoyed your afternoon. I must tell you that the board have considered your company's proposals. They thank you for your frankness but they regret that they do not wish to be associated with your new bid nor do they wish to sell the company's holding in Blenders. Sonkay still hopes that Forde Jamieson will use its shares to support the present management of Blenders in solving its problems and look forward to co-operating with you."

"Thank you, Mr Saginuma. I quite understand the position and shall be in touch with you when I have reported to my Board."

Frank's hands were clammy with relief when he returned to James. "I wonder how narrow a squeak that was. I think the finance director was quite tempted."

"What do you mean?"

"When I saw them this morning I asked them to join in a new bid at 380p a share or, alternatively, to sell us their shares at 380p."

"Good God! What new bid?"

"There isn't one. And we certainly couldn't afford to pay 380p a share."

"What if your bluff had been called?"

"I suppose I should have had to commit the City equivalent of hara kiri – go and write children's books or do social work. But it wasn't and it means that Sarah has got a good price for her shares."

"What about Forde Jamieson's shares?"

"That's my problem," said Frank ruefully. "I suppose I saw this in a sense as a modern variation on the mediaeval conflict between love and duty, my love for Sarah and my duty to the bank. But, of course, in practice, these things are never so simple. Securing a fortune for Sarah, whom I hope to marry, could be construed as self-love and a betrayal of trust in order to line one's own pocket. Against that, there are elementary considerations of justice, or, if you like, fair play for innocent bystanders. Sarah has already suffered one terrible wrong in the loss of her father: as a contestant in the struggle which caused this I could be said to have a duty to make sure that she does not also suffer financially as well. I don't suppose Tim will see it in that light, though. You don't get where he has by being over-scrupulous."

"There could be a way round this," said James. "I could always get the remaining 5 per cent I need from you, I suppose, but there may be a better answer still. Let me think about it. Meanwhile, I'm going to order some champagne. I want to drink a toast to you and Sarah: you're very fortunate in each other. Then you and I will go to Roppongi and eat Kobé beef 'Teppan Yaki', that means cooked in thin strips on a hot metal plate. The Japanese don't live only on raw fish and seaweed. Kobé cattle are said to be raised on beer: whether they are or not, it's the most delicious meat in the world."

On Thursday, James and Frank checked in together at Narita airport for the sixteen-hour flight to London. Shortly after they were airborne, James turned to Frank, "I have been thinking a lot about Andrew's killing. Let's see if we can get any further by going over the ground again. I grant you that Sonkay could be said to have had a motive – they wanted to prevent Forde Jamieson getting control. But after meeting them on their home ground, I am totally convinced that they would never have involved themselves in murder, otherwise I could not have sold them Sarah's shares. Corporate executives don't hire killers. Why should they take the risk? That, as we said, is the reaction of an entrepreneur playing for high stakes. Therefore, we eliminate the Japanese. Now, who else was desperate to prevent Forde Jamieson getting Andrew's shares?"

"We agreed," Frank responded, "that Dougal ranked as desperate, as he knew his empire would be liquidated by us and he would be for the chop. But I am sure the name Itsuki Fujioka meant nothing to him and he didn't have the resources – or indeed the wit – to employ go-betweens to insulate him. There must be another angle. Who else involved is desperate and has the mentality, resources and contacts to stage Andrew's death?"

"Of course," erupted James, "but of course. How could I be so blind? Joseph Mabalian. That *is* someone who fits that bill exactly – an entrepreneur with everything to lose. But because he's been on the sidelines so far we've overlooked him. Mabalian . . ."

"The Likkermart man?"

"Yes. Don't you see how it all fits together? If you had got control of Blenders he knew you would use every trick in the book, and perhaps a few not in it as well, to get round Blenders' contract with Likkermart. And it's that contract which has pushed Likkermart's share price from \$5 to \$25, making him a millionaire many times over. In addition, this is something you couldn't have known, he wanted to mount a takeover bid for Blenders using Likkermart shares underwritten by a group of West Coast operators."

"He'd never have got away with that," scoffed Frank.

"I'm not so sure. There's a lot of money on the West Coast and if they had got a half-way reputable house to act for them, it could well have worked on institutions wondering what on earth to do with their Blenders: the offer of stock in a high-flying US company, with a cash alternative, would have been pretty attractive. Mabalian would have offered the Board service contracts, and, if the Japanese had not come to the rescue, I am sure they would in the end have preferred a marriage with Likkermart to rape by Forde Jamieson. That's why he had to prevent you getting control of Andrew's shares."

"How would he have known about our deal with Andrew?"

"I was at the meeting," said James, "when Andrew told the board, which, of course, included Dougal, and I assume Dougal, who seems pretty thick with Mabalian, told him. It's odd: I believe there wasn't much love lost between Mabalian and Dougal when Dougal realised what a bad deal he'd made. But then he seems to have decided that, as he had alienated the rest of the Board, his best hope of an ally lay in Mabalian, which I suppose is why he was so keen to promote the merger."

"Have you met Mabalian?"

"Only once and I can't say I took to him. He was staying in one of the most expensive suites in Grosvenor House. Perhaps I was prejudiced by gossip about his Mafia and gangster connections but he struck me as brash and second-rate – certainly not the sort of person with whom Braithwaites would want to do business. I'm not sure of his origins. Although he is Americanised now, I believe he came from somewhere between Turkey and the Lebanon originally."

"And did Andrew go into the details of the option he had given us?"

"Yes: I remember him stressing that the option was good for his lifetime only."

"So Dougal would almost certainly have told his ally, Mabalian, of this obstacle. And Mabalian probably asked Dougal Andrew's movements over the next few days, saying he might want to get in touch with him directly."

"That would have seemed innocent enough at the time. And I remember Andrew mentioning also at the board meeting that he was going to Bormona."

"Which would have given Mabalian time to get on to his underworld network. He may well have had links with the PLO and they would have led him straight to Fujioka. Now that I think of it, I remember Fujioka saying that he had done work for the Arab powers."

"Let's see where we've got to, Frank." James was thoughtful. "We have established an interesting circumstantial hypothesis, but at the moment we haven't got anything that could even be called circumstantial evidence. On the other hand, I cannot see that there is anybody else for whom we could even begin to construct such an hypothesis. That means this is the only track we can follow at the moment: the trouble is that it's going to be the devil's own job to pin anything on him. In fact, though, I've made a start. After I saw him at Grosvenor House, I asked associates of ours in Chicago to check him out for us. When we get back to London I'll see what they've come up with. Until then I don't think there is a great deal more we can do."

"I shall have problems of my own when we get back," observed Frank wryly.

"Ah yes. Those unsold Blenders' shares. The solution to the two problems could be interconnected: a plan is beginning to take shape at the back of my mind, but much depends on how we get on with Mr Mabalian."

At this stage minute hostesses with large, permanently fixed smiles arrived with lunch trays. Frank, whose appetite had been stimulated by the mental exercise, lifted the lid off his plate in anticipation. "Oh no," he groaned, looking at the exquisitely arranged slivers of raw fish, "not again."

"Never mind," said James cheerfully, who was aware of an incipient weight problem. "After Moscow the food usually gets more homely."

CHAPTER XXI

Although Frank followed carefully the seasoned traveller's precepts – light slippers, loose clothes, no alcohol – long aircraft journeys made him nervy and frustrated. Waking with a thick head and rough tongue, he lurched towards the queue for the aircraft's cupboard-sized lavatories and observed with some satisfaction that Orientals appeared to find air travel equally arduous. The ranks of distorted figures propped in the narrow economy seats looked like survivors from a terrorist outrage rather than expectant tourists. But maybe even this, reflected Frank, might be better than life in a Japanese factory. In truth, for he did not like to admit to romantic hankerings, he cherished a fondness for the thought of the old flying boats of Imperial Airways where the passengers sat in armchairs and slept in hotels each night en route to the East: as the resurrected Orient Express appeared to be a success, maybe this would be the next development in luxury leisure. He was awoken from this entrepreneurial daydream by the door tugging open as a spruce Japanese businessman, hair lacquered back, rotary badge in position and grin fixed for the day, emerged. Frank entered, cursed his own shortsightedness in not bringing soap, washed his teeth in lukewarm water, shaved hopefully with his electric razor, shook the plastic after-shave bottle to make sure that it was indeed empty, dried with a coarse paper towel and feeling nevertheless somewhat more buoyant, returned to his seat. James's report that they had passed Frankfurt and something akin to an English breakfast was on its way, further revived him.

"Sleep well?" asked Frank.

"As well as can be expected. I never do in these things. But it's given me an opportunity to think about the problem of your unsold shares. I can see a possible answer, which would have the additional merit of an element of poetic justice. But the timetable may be fine. Under the takeover rules, we have to announce the sale of Sarah's shares and Sonkay's purchases by noon the day after we deal: you can imagine the effect that will have on the price, particularly as Sonkay have asked us to announce at the same time that they will use their 29 per cent to support the Board and have no intention either of increasing their holding further, or making a bid."

Frank thought briefly. "With Sonkay no longer a buyer, but in a position to block our or any other bid, I should think the price would probably halve as the punters pile out."

"That sounds to be about right. Ah, here's food."

The promised English breakfast turned out to be the usual airborne travesty: the sausages were skinless, the eggs solid and the bacon overcrisped: instead of toast there were cold croissants and the coffee was watery. But Frank became so engrossed in the unfolding of James's plan that he, at least, failed to notice.

"Now," continued James, "although I have Sonkay's bank draft with me, I haven't actually dealt in Sarah's shares yet. Also I have to pick up another 5 per cent of Blenders to get to the 29 per cent. That's not a problem in itself. I only need to hint to a couple of pension funds that I think the price has gone too far and they'll sell on the spot. And there are a couple to whom we owe a good turn. Alternatively, I could bid you for some of your holding but the 12 per cent you would be left with would be a much less strategic block and the plan I have in mind demands a strategic block. Will you run a commercial risk with me, Frank?"

"Of course."

"Good. Then I shall go and rest when we reach London, claiming age and jet lag, and not reach the office until after lunch by which time I should have spoken to the pension funds. I shall put the shares through the market then which gives me until Monday noon to make the announcement – and gives you until then to place your holding."

"How? The market wouldn't take it."

"I wouldn't let you place it in the market and allow innocent people to suffer."

"If not innocent, then who?" Frank paused. "Oh, of course, Mabalian. I am slow this morning."

"I think it must be the breakfast," said James wryly. "Now we both know he wants to bid for Blenders and I know he has been trying to get his hands on a block as a launching pad. Dougal sounded me out discreetly on Sarah's shares, saying Mabalian had the cash available. I must confess I stonewalled. Something made me uneasy: maybe I was just beginning to have my suspicions even then. In any event, apart from the fact that I trusted the Japanese more, I was sure Andrew would not have wanted his shares to go to Likkermart. But I am sure he would be delighted for them to have yours at the wrong price." James paused, slightly embarrassed. "This is, of course, all most unprofessional and I'm not sure that Forde Jamieson deserve to be let off the hook, particularly after the Luke episode. But you have behaved with great generosity in Tokyo and I think it is owed to you personally."

A barely intelligible sing-song interrupted: "We are now commencing our descent to Heathrow airport. Will passengers fasten their seat belts, extinguish their cigarettes and make sure their seats are in the upright position."

"Thank God for that," said James. "I don't think I could have sat through another hour of this."

Sarah was at the barrier to meet them. "The two men of whom I am fondest. How lovely to see you together."

"Well, it's thanks to him you still rank as an heiress," James spoke fondly as he hugged Sarah.

"How marvellous. I'm dying to hear all about it. But let's get back to the car first."

On the crowded M4 motorway to London Sarah listened intently to James's version of events in Tokyo. She said gently, "Frank, you didn't have to do that for me – you might have wrecked your whole career."

"You've suffered much more," said Frank simply. "If my bluff had been called I could always have found another job eventually. But nothing will bring your father back."

Sarah took one hand off the steering wheel to squeeze Frank's.

"Forde Jamieson's unsold shares, all 17 million of them, are the remaining problem," said James, "but there may be a way of solving that too." He then sketched the idea of selling the Forde Jamieson shares to Mabalian.

"I can't think in a balanced way about my father's murderer: I just want to batter his head in and I shan't be happy until he's behind bars, preferably waiting for the hangman if we still had one. In the meantime, let's do to him what damage we can, particularly if, in this case, it's going to help Frank also. How shall we approach Mabalian without arousing his suspicions?"

"It might be a bit difficult for me," said James thoughtfully. "He knew I wasn't keen on this bid and he might smell a rat."

"I know," said Sarah, "why don't I get in touch with Dougal? We know he gets straight on to Mabalian. Frank can scarcely approach Dougal after their blazing row at the funeral, but there's no reason why I shouldn't. I'll call from the office which will make it more convincing as Leo Hudson is working for Blenders. I'll say that we've heard from the market that the Forde Jamieson bid is in trouble as they haven't been able to get Daddy's shares. I'll say, that's it, that I've got the impression from Frank that Forde Jamieson want a quick out and are ready to do a deal. What's more, I'll say as Frank has been in Tokyo it looks as though they're talking to Sonkay – you know how Dougal hates the

Japanese – and I'm calling him because that would obviously put Sonkay in a strong position to make a bid and my father would never have wanted the Japanese to control Blenders, and can he stop it? How does that sound?"

"That's a juicy bait," said James, "I'll be surprised if he doesn't rise to that. Meanwhile, I'll see what more I can find out about Mr Mabalian."

Frank showered, changed, had a cup of proper coffee and, when he arrived on Friday mid-morning at Forde Jamieson's, went straight to see Tim.

"Welcome back. How did you get on?"

"Nothing definite yet, I'm afraid. The Japanese were very courteous, listened carefully and asked sensible questions. They said they would let me know, but I have a hunch they may be trying to deal elsewhere."

"What do you mean?"

"Well, I bumped into James Murray from Braithwaites out there. He's Sarah's godfather and we'd met at the funeral. He seemed a bit embarrassed at meeting me again and was very cagey about what he was up to. I took him out and gave him a few drinks, and then a few more, but he still wouldn't say a word although he did loosen up about other things." (Frank offered a silent apology to the abstemious and discreet James.) "He told me a very interesting story about our dealings with Luke Grey." Tim flushed at this revelation. "But more importantly let slip that Likkermart have the cash backing to make a bid. They haven't got a shareholding yet and while the Japanese are going through the agonising process of making up their corporate minds, I want to sound out Mr Mabalian."

"That seems sensible." Tim made no comment on Luke. "But we must be incredibly discreet. If the market were to get a hint we're sellers, the price would collapse."

"Don't worry, I've got a most trustworthy intermediary. I'll keep you in touch."

Back in his own office Frank had barely begun on the accumulation in his in-tray when Sarah telephoned:

"I think it's worked. Dougal got very excited. It seems that Joseph Mabalian is back in England and they want you to meet them for lunch today in Mabalian's suite at Grosvenor House. But I've told Dougal he's got to apologise to you."

Frank relished the vulgarity of the suite – pink lampshades and overcut crystal goblets – which made an admirable setting for Mabalian's fleshy, dark looks. "I bet he's as much Turk as Armenian," thought Frank, "put him with a fez on his head in a room full of carved mirrors and cushions and he'd make a perfect pasha. He's ruthless enough and probably sadistic as well."

Dougal, spruce, neat, his greying hair close-cut, advanced to meet Frank. "Mr Higgins, I'm so glad to meet you again. It gives me the opportunity to apologise for that unfortunate misunderstanding at poor Andrew's funeral last week."

"I thought we understood each other very well," said Frank blandly, "but let's say no more of it. We have more important matters to discuss today."

"You are right, Mr Higgins." Joseph Mabalian's voice was deep, guttural and still slightly accented by his origins. "But before we talk business, shall we order lunch? I recommend the caviare."

"That's a recommendation I'm always happy to follow. Then I'll have a tournedos, medium rare, if I may." Dougal nodded assent and Mabalian barked into the telephone, "Three Beluga, three tournedos medium rare, a bottle of Taittinger '66 and a Latour '61. And be quick."

"Well, Mr Higgins, now that's done, let's discuss our mutual interests. I understand that Forde Jamieson may not press ahead with its bid for Blenders."

"Unfortunately, we have lost a block of stock which we believed was committed to us." (At this Mabalian shot a brief glance at Dougal.) "Without it we are not really in a strong enough position to press ahead and sadly we have not the resources on our own to take on Sonkay. I say sadly because we are convinced there is tremendous potential still in Blenders and we don't like the thought that it will be the Japanese who exploit it. Sarah MacLintock is very much against our selling to the Japanese as she still feels they may have been responsible for her father's death but it looks as though we have no alternative."

"We've got to keep the yellow bastards out whatever happens. Let them make their own malt if they're so clever." Dougal's vindictiveness was unabated.

"I think you may have an alternative, Mr Higgins." Joseph Mabalian smiled happily as he ran his fingers through his thick hair in sheer pleasure at the turn of events. "I have preferred to watch progress from the sidelines. It is often better to let others tire themselves in the battle before joining in. Do you not think so, Mr Higgins?"

"Yes, indeed." Frank decided to play up to the role of the small-time operator who had got out of his league.

"Ah, here is lunch." His host, exuding commercial charm, piled the caviare on to Frank's plate. "It is magnificent, the Beluga. The grains are as precious as black pearls, as rare to the taste as the honey from Mount Athos. When I was a little village boy in Anatolia I never dreamt that I would one day sit in London's best hotel eating caviare by the plateful. We should drink to that, Mr Higgins, to life's unexpected surprises."

"I should be delighted to. I am a great believer in life's unexpected surprises."

"How well the champagne goes with the caviare. The bubbles complement the grains. Caviare from Russia, champagne from France. It is the true marriage of East and West. But now," Mabalian, abandoning fantasy, put down his spoon reluctantly, "I take it, Mr Higgins, that you would like us to buy your holding in Blenders?"

"I want to sell our holding in Blenders: you are one of a number of possible buyers. There are the Japanese, and while we respect the MacLintock family's scruples, we cannot be bound by them. Then there is the London Stock Market. As soon as it is known that you are interested as well as the Japanese we should have no difficulty selling there. I think our position is interesting and that a key block like this should command a premium over the market price, which this morning was 375p."

"A premium! I like your British sense of humour, Mr Higgins. I can see why it is famous. But you are not serious."

"Perfectly. I am sure the Japanese would pay a premium. Together with what they have, it would assure them control. And the market price, as I said, will rise when your interest is known."

"No, no. I will not pay a premium. Joseph Mabalian has never paid the same price as the crowd in the bazaar – that is why we are able to eat caviare today."

"Well then, let me offer a compromise. We'll agree the middle market price, but will deal directly with each other. That cuts out the brokers' commissions and the jobber's 'turn' – that's the difference between the buying and selling price. In that case, you pay less and I receive more."

"I agree. Let us drink to that."

"Well done," said Dougal, "well done," looking as pleased as a midwife who had herself given birth.

Frank broke in, "As we're dealing this way, it must be done on a cash basis. I have signed transfer forms here with me: Mr Mabalian, can you let me have a banker's draft?"

"Within the hour: I shall telephone now for it to be sent."

"Good. And could you please make it two drafts. One a small one, say, £50,000, made out to the Commonwealth Tobacco Co Sponsorship a/c, and the major one, which I calculate at £63,700,000 to Forde Jamieson. You will appreciate, of course, that under the takeover rules we shall have to announce this sale?"

"Of course. Let us announce simultaneously so that we can declare our bid at the same time. I must discuss the terms this weekend with my backers and the New York bank which will make the offer. Can you hold the announcement until Monday?"

"Noon at the latest."

"I'll meet that deadline. Now, for that drink. Dougal be so good as to order another bottle of champagne for us."

"There you are," said Frank, putting the drafts on Tim Weston's desk, "there's still time to bank ours before the weekend."

"What on earth is this £50,000 to the Commonwealth Tobacco Sponsorship Fund?"

"You might call it conscience money. It's to be used to sponsor that theatre group in California which has taken on Luke Grey's young friend. I thought it would be appropriate for our name to appear as sponsors."

"What did Tim Weston say to that?" Sarah was laughing so hard that tears started to her eyes. James, to whose St Leonard's Terrace house they had gone for an early evening drink, joined in the merriment.

"I wonder what on earth old Ron Pheasant at Commonwealth will make of it. He'll think Weston is after a knighthood and put him on the Council of the Confederation of British Industry if he's not careful. Serve him right, too. Now, my dears, I must leave you. Clarissa has been in the country all week while I was in Japan and she's expecting me for a late dinner tonight. I shall need a good rest in the country to get my strength up for Monday, which promises to be an interesting day. You must be feeling pretty whacked, too, Frank."

"Actually I seem to be getting a second wind."

"In which case it can blow us towards a good dinner," said Sarah.

"What about the Thomas de Quincey?"

"Ummy," said Sarah, suddenly looking like a very little girl.

* * *

"I believe the salmon quenelles here are the most delicious form of fish there is." Sarah spoke dreamily as they sat in Convent Garden's most agreeable restaurant.

"It's difficult for those of us who had Beluga caviare for lunch to judge."

"Pig. But I love you."

"Eat up. They say fish stimulates the carnal desires."

"Mine don't need stimulating. I've been aching for you all week. Frank, is it awful, longing for you so much so soon after my poor father's death?"

"Nothing will bring Andrew back now. And he wouldn't want you to be unhappy."

"I suppose not. But I hate that man, Mabalian, that villain, that smiling, damned villain. I want to go and kill him with my own hands. I should like to bash his head in with an axe. I don't think I could control myself if I met him. We can't let him get away with it. Frank, what are we going to do about it? Can't we go to the police?"

"They could never prove the connection to Fujioka. We must operate in our own way. To begin with, we've set him up to be at least £21 million poorer by Monday afternoon. Those 17 million shares he bought from us at 375p won't be worth more than 250p after the Sonkay announcement on Monday. Maybe less. His company hasn't got the £64 million he paid us. That will have to come from his backers who, I believe, are to be found mainly in Las Vegas. They don't like to lose a third of that sort of money over a weekend. They might yet do your job for you – except I believe they favour concrete."

"What a nice thought."

"Now, unless you eat up and take me home quickly, I'm not going to be able to do anything about your carnal aches. The flight's beginning to catch up with me."

"Let's skip the coffee and get the bill now."

CHAPTER XXII

On Monday morning Frank telephoned James. "What time are you making the Sonkay purchase announcement? At 11.45. Good. Then I'll tell our agency to put this announcement out at 11.55 precisely:

> 'Forde Jamieson & Company Limited announce they have sold 17 million shares in Blenders to Likkermart Inc at a price of 375p a share.
> 'Likkermart Inc announce that it has bought 17 million shares in Blenders from Forde Jamieson at a price of 375p. It intends to make a share exchange offer underwritten for cash at the equivalent of 375p a share for the remaining shares of Blenders. The offer is conditional upon Likkermart gaining a 75 per cent level of acceptance.'

Their New York bankers obviously insist upon 75 per cent as they need that to be able to alter the Articles of Association. What will your announcement say Sonkay has?"

James chuckled, "The magic 29 per cent – which means that Mabalian's bid is lost before he makes it."

At 11.45 precisely Braithwaites' statement was posted on the board of the Stock Exchange and flashed simultaneously on to the City's television screens:

> "Braithwaite & Company have sold 10,000,000 shares in Blenders on behalf of a discretionary client and 6,800,000 on behalf of other clients at 369½p. They have bought a

total of 16,800,000 shares for Sonkay Ltd of Japan at 370p. Sonkay have authorised Braithwaite & Company to state that it now holds 29 per cent of Blenders equity. It is the policy of Sonkay to use this holding to support the Blenders' Board. Sonkay will not be acquiring any more shares in Blenders in the market nor will it make a bid for the Blenders' shares it does not already own."

The impact on the Blenders' price was immediate and drastic. The three jobbers who dealt in the shares marked it down at once to 250p. A scrum around the jobbers' stands thickened as the market's thwarted speculators rushed to cut their losses and red pencils marked the price on down – 240p, 230p, 225p. James who had brought Frank to the visitors' gallery to watch said, "You realise this is mostly the market punters dealing on their own account. The word won't have reached the public yet. That'll give the price another bang when they come in."

Frank said, "Look, I think the second announcement has gone up." From their vantage point they saw the crowd surge away from the jobbers and throng around the announcement board. The crowd read once, read a second time, puzzled looks were exchanged, quick conference taken, then almost unanimously came the verdict – peals of derisive laughter. "Well, the market got the message clearly enough," observed James. "Now, you'd better come back to my office. We can have some quiet lunch and when Dougal and his nasty crony turn up to rant about my Sonkay deal, as I don't doubt they will, I'll lend you a tin hat."

James and Frank were alone just after 2 o'clock when the Braithwaite porter telephoned. "Mr Fordson's here, Mr Murray, with another gentleman. They say they must see you urgently. I said I thought you were at lunch but they say they'll wait anyhow."

"That's all right, Sandelson, send them up to the small luncheon room."

Dougal, his face flushed even redder than it had been at Andrew's funeral, burst into the room a minute later with Mabalian at his heels.

"Good Christ," he shouted on seeing Frank, "what are you doing here?" Comprehension dawned, "You're in this together. You've set us up."

"I can't think what you are shouting about, Dougal," James spoke with maddening calmness. "Mr Higgins and I indeed are in something together. He is engaged – albeit unofficially – to marry my goddaughter Sarah, and as I am the executor of her father's will, we were discussing her financial situation. But it's essentially a family matter."

"Then it was Andrew's shares you sold to the bloody Nips. You let Andrew's murderers have his shares. Are you crazy? It beggars belief. On top of that you're Blenders' broker, too. Why didn't you consult the Board? I'll go to the Stock Exchange and the Takeover Panel. Just wait till I speak to the newspapers. You and your precious ethics and good name. You're a bucket shop run by swindlers and you should be exposed."

"I think you should both begin by sitting down." James indicated two chairs. "To take your minor accusation first, I was acting in my capacity as Andrew's executor with a responsibility to get the best possible price when I sold. I discussed the matter with the chairman this morning and he was most pleased with the deal. It makes Blenders bidproof until trading recovers and, meanwhile, Sonkay can be of great assistance in many of Blenders' export markets."

"But they're murderers. You sold shares to murderers."

"I left it to Frank here to do that."

The nine-word sentence hung in the air like a slowly lobbed hand grenade.

Dougal exploded, "You're not just a twister, Murray, you're mad. Stark, staring, raving mad."

"No, I just think more logically than you, and I don't jump to the first conclusion that appears." James remained unruffled. Frank was watching Mabalian who was looking straight ahead, apparently detached from Dougal's outbursts. "Andrew's murder was admittedly carried out by a Japanese, but that did not mean that he was acting for Sonkay. There are, after all, a hundred and fifteen million Japanese and they don't all work for Sonkay. Andrew's killer, Itsuki Fujioka, was employed by your associate, Joseph Mabalian."

Mabalian's features tightened momentarily at the mention of Fujioka's name, but he swiftly said, "What new madness is this? I have no idea what you are talking about."

"I am surprised you say that," said Frank softly, "Fujioka boasted to me of the killing and told me how you had paid half into the Credit Suisse beforehand."

"That's the normal arrangement," Mabalian barked, his composure punctured.

James pounced, "You have frequent dealings with Mr Fujioka then and his associates?"

Mabalian recovered quickly, "I've told you I don't know what you are talking about. I just meant that it's well known that those are the usual terms for people like that. This is all hearsay and ridiculous. There is nothing to be gained by sitting here listening to wild accusations from common tricksters. Dougal, let's go."

"Not so fast, Joseph. I want to hear some more about this. I still have scruples and I am certainly not prepared to be associated with Andrew's murderer."

"I think you'll find Andrew's murder is not the only crime in Joseph Mabalian's book," cut in James. "The FBI are investigating the arson of a hotel in Las Vegas run by one of his business rivals. Nine people died in that fire and there are witnesses to say that it was started by an Oriental who answers Fujioka's description."

"Shit. America is full of Mafiosi. Why should it be anything to do with me?"

"At the moment there is no connection. But Frank's hearsay would link you decisively to it. The evidence might not stand up in a court of law – you're too wily for that, Mr

Mabalian, but the authorities have other ways of working. I don't believe you've got your full United States citizenship yet, have you Mr Mabalian?"

"How do you know? It's nothing to do with you." The composure was crumbling.

"My sources are good. It's important in this business. So, if we pass the information on to the FBI, that you employed Fujioka as an assassin and we are people whose word carries weight, we know who to tell, you can expect opposition to your citizenship and difficulties in the renewal of your liquor licences. In other words, Mr Mabalian, the end of your American dream. I think you're a bit old to start again in Brazil. I doubt you have the energy, you've lived too well."

A knock at the door lowered the tension. Milo put his head round and said, "James, Blenders down to 155p."

"Thanks Milo. Better do as we said."

"Fair enough."

"What price?" shrieked Mabalian, his voice torn with fear and fury.

"155p," said James calmly.

"Then I have lost over 70 million dollars today."

"In round numbers, that sounds about right," said Frank cheerfully.

Mabalian's face dropped into his hands.

"I get the impression," said James, "that you may have more to fear in the short run from your backers in Las Vegas than from the FBI. From my knowledge they don't take kindly to losses of this size in so short a space of time and their reactions can be brutal. May I make a suggestion to you, Mr Mabalian? If you tear up that unfortunate contract you made with Dougal, which caused Blenders' problems in the first case, I can assure you that the share price would bound back to 250p at least, possibly more. Your friends might just stomach that loss. But if you don't cancel it, I'll personally see that the price gets down to 100p tonight, and that would bring your loss up to 90 million dollars."

"But what about Likkermart?"

"You own most of the shares. The problem, and the choice, is yours."

A low moan escaped through the fingers covering Mabalian's face. There was a long pause, then the head nodded slowly.

"Dougal, will you take your murderous friend to your solicitors and sort out the formalities. Let me know just as soon as he's signed. It must be announced at once."

That night there was a family dinner party in St Leonard's Terrace to mark Sarah's engagement. Marina, composed in black, raised her glass and said, "I know Andrew would have been delighted about this, and I am too. But I think we must observe the formalities, say nothing in public for at least two months." General agreement was nodded.

"We shall miss Andrew," said James ruefully. "He was a dear friend. The one place where Frank can replace him, though, is on the Blenders board."

"What are you talking about, James? I've got nothing to do with Blenders now. And as you sold Sarah's shares to the Japanese it isn't as though she has any that need representation."

"Actually, she has," said James, smiling. "When the price panicked to 150p this afternoon I was able to buy back 6 million of her 10 million shares. The arithmetic is simple. We got £37 million from the Japanese on which we owe the taxman nearly £28 million, leaving Sarah with just over £9 million of free capital – enough to buy 6 million shares.

"That's what you told Milo to do," exclaimed Frank.

James nodded happily, "You will recollect that at that point I had not proposed to Mabalian to tear up the agreement, so I cannot be said to have acted on inside information – perhaps an outside hunch." He continued, "With 6 per cent of the company Sarah is still the biggest shareholder after the Japanese and her holding merits representation.

Apart from that I have formed a high opinion of Frank's shrewdness and resourcefulness: with Sonkay's backing he could make Blenders the success it should be. I think the Company will be lucky to have him, and the chairman, to whom I spoke this afternoon, agrees."

"But they're Sarah's shares, not mine. She should be on the board," objected Frank.

"Well spoken, darling," said Sarah. "But for the time being, just let me be your alternate."

Six months later, at breakfast in Oxfordshire, Clarissa suddenly looked up from her *Sunday Star*, "Isn't this the man you were involved with? 'Mysterious death of entrepreneur. Police in Nevada are investigating the drowning in Lake Tahoe of liquor millionaire, Joseph Mabalian, who briefly hit the headlines in Britain with an abortive bid for Blenders. He was seen playing in Harrah's Casino earlier in the evening but was not seen leaving it.' "

"Maybe the syndicate couldn't stand the loss after all."

"What *are* you talking about, James?"

"Just a man whose luck deservedly ran out."